The Figure on the Boundary Line

Mahul E 1972   20/25

CHRISTOPH MECKEL

The Figure
on the Boundary Line

SELECTED PROSE

edited by Christopher Middleton

Graphics by the Author
Translations by Christopher Middleton,
Brian Harris and Margaret Woodruff

CARCANET PRESS/MANCHESTER

First published in Great Britain in 1983 by
Carcanet New Press Ltd
208–212 Corn Exchange Buildings
Manchester M4 3BQ

ISBN 0 85635 400 7

Meckel, Christoph
   The figure on the boundary line
   1. German prose literature
   I. Title
   838'.91408   PT2673.E28

   ISBN 0-85635-400-7

The publisher acknowledges the financial assistance of the Arts Council
of Great Britain.

Typeset by Paragon Photoset, Aylesbury
Printed in England by Short Run Press Ltd, Exeter

Contents

Translations of the early short prose pieces, from
'Ucht' to 'End of the World', also 'Tullipan', are by
Brian Harris; translations of 'Zünd' and 'Crow' are
by Margaret Woodruff; the remaining texts were
translated by Christopher Middleton.

Acknowledgements

Acknowledgement is made to the editors of the following publications in which some of the translations appeared previously: *Dimension, Invisible City, Penguin German Writing Today, PN Review, Willow Springs Magazine.*

German sources are as follows: *Manifest der Toten* (Eremiten-Presse, 1960, rev.1971); 'Ucht' from 'Anstelle eines Vorworts' in *Im Lande der Umbramauten* (Deutsche Verlags-Anstalt, 1961); 'Inventions', 'Prospect' and 'Tower Theatre' from 'Erfindungen' in *Im Lande*; 'Tear Animals', 'The Hotel', 'Baan', 'My Friends' and 'End of the World' from 'Begebenheiten' in *Im Lande*; 'The Lion' in the miscellany *Beispiele* (1962); *Tullipan* (Verlag Klaus Wagenbach, 1965); 'Zünd' in *Neue Rundschau* (1964); 'The Crow' in the miscellany *Das Atelier* (1962); 'Gulliver's Death' in *Merkur* (1966); 'An Unpleasant Story' in *Dimension* (1968); 'Workshop Notes' in *Bilderbotschaften* (1969); 'Felicitation' and 'The Negro's Story' in *Werkauswahl* (Nymphenburger Verlagshandlung, 1971); 'Tunifer's Memories' in *Dimension* (1973); *Die Gestalt am Ende des Grundstücks* (Eremiten-Presse, 1975); 'Wissen Sie wie Caravaggio gestorben ist?', author's typescript, 1979.

The graphics were selected by Christoph Meckel and are not associated with any specific text.

Editor's Preface

This selection covers twenty years of Christoph Meckel's shorter prose. Until recently, much of his work was published by German small presses, and in fairly small editions. Translations into English have appeared sporadically in magazines, but precious little has been known of his stupendous graphic work, etchings and drawings; even in the German Federal Republic, recognition of his achievement as a writer-artist in the grand fantastic tradition has been quite slow in coming.

Yet in Meckel's background there have always been ancestors, remote like Niklaus Manuel, or more recent, like Kokoschka, or Schwitters, or Arp; and in his own time there have been several noted double talents, one of whom, the lamented Günter Bruno Fuchs, was a friend and ally of Meckel's. It seems that the German public of the last twenty-five years has tended to prefer astute father-figure writers to incorrigible son-figures like Meckel. To probe a little deeper, few have been able to detect in Meckel a sort of Dionysian *puer aeternus*, who combines a set of volatile visionary impulses, ranging from the apocalyptic to the whimsical, with 'technical' skills of his own invention — skills that are very diverse, but also unique, mature, and altogether masterful.

Some of this charactered diversity, but only some, may be perceptible in the present selection. For the English-speaking reader, who may be encountering Meckel for the first time here, an appreciation of the broader picture will be aided if I mention that there are now twelve narrative-pictorial cycles of etchings (1959–82), each comprising about fifty pictures, and that Meckel now regards this 'Human Comedy' as complete. There are also over a dozen books of texts accompanied by graphics (1956, f. — etchings, linocuts,

colour prints). There are ten or more books of poems (1956–
79), and as many of shorter prose. Recently, too, there have
been books of a memorial kind: a memoir of the poet
Johannes Bobrowski (1978), a memoir of Meckel's father
(*Suchbild*, 1980); in a related vein, but as a study of an
exemplary Russian poet, *Nachricht für Baratynski* (1981), and
as a kind of fantastic fictional self-study (I believe), *Der wahre
Muftoni* (1982). Two books which resemble novels are
Bockshorn (1973) and *Licht* (1978); but rather than spell out
the substances of such literary texts I would rather round out
this set of indications by referring to the several brilliant
cycles of coloured drawings, done in pencil, gouache and
chalk, which even Meckel has lost count of — each cycle
comprises twelve or fifteen items: we have here, perhaps,
some of the most luminous lyrical creations that have come
out of Meckel's explosive yet very delicate imagination.

The one epithet that could be applied to his work as a
whole — and it is a consistent and coherent *oeuvre* in every
respect — is *exuberant*. Three times, if I may sound a personal
note, Meckel and I have worked together on big graphic/
lyrical folios, each with about a dozen sheets. We did the first
book here in River Hills, Texas, on a trestle-table behind my
house on a sunny Spring day in 1968, and we called it
Misthauf Gackeltons Gugelfuhr — the title means,
approximately, though the anagrams are lost in translation,
Dunghill Roostercall's Follywagon. The second book we did
on the floor during a rainy summer day, also in 1968, in the
ruined cottage where Meckel used to spend his Vaucluse
times: we called it *The Rain Book (Das Regenbuch)*. The third
book was again done on a table, this time in Berlin, in
December 1978, and we called it *Das Buch vom chronischen
Mumpiz — The Book of Chronic Stuff and Nonsense*. Each
sheet was adorned with improvised poems, drawings,
collages, and quotations (real or imaginary). Some sheets we
worked on simultaneously, or at least jointly. Each book has
its own singular style (never settled in advance); formally
speaking, the first two are less classically spare and severe
than the third, but all carry the rhythmic movement of
Meckel's exuberance, even where my workings, more
groping and more slow, were touched by it.

Then again the reader of this selection will find that

Meckel's inventive exuberance has its deep tensions and its
dark aspects. He was born in 1935 in Berlin: he was in Erfurt
as a ten-year-old evacuee when in 1945 the ravaged town
repeatedly changed hands between Russian and American
troops, and when a single frost-bitten potato was an object of
epicurean reverence. As an artist he is largely self-taught, and
he has been a freelance since the age of twenty, travelling
much of the world, except the Near and Far East. He has
endured hardships no worse than many have; but his ill-
health since 1969, when, after two major operations, he
tested his chances by etching his cycle *Der Strom (The River)*,
would have annihilated most. There is in his nature something wild, something resistant, which creates against
mortality, against the averagings of inertia, and in the teeth of
despair. (His 'Caravaggio' might seem extravagant in its
rhetoric, but in that prose he has nailed his own questions.)
In his work, as in his tenacity as an artist, one might find an
interesting qualification of what Freya Stark wrote with
regard to her own independence and her own impulses: 'The
wild soul is perhaps conscious . . . of the intrinsic danger of
life, which is hidden from the domesticated, whether animal
or human . . . it does not do to assume the domestic alone to
be laudable in a world where all the chances of survival are
with wildness' *(Beyond Euphrates* (1951) pp. 62–3).

For the sake of coherence and succinctness I have not
included in the selection any translations of Meckel's poems.
There is one poem, however, which will serve to introduce it
more immediately than any amount of detail I can offer. The
poem is called 'Talking about Poetry' and it is dated 1968:

We have toppled
the tree, have chased
the tree through autumn,
have hung it with hailstones and snow:

we have dried the rivers
and counted the water,
have held the wave up to the light,
and have weighed the flow
in the fountain:

we thought we could capture
the owl, feathers it shed
was all we held, we copied
the owl's talk in our language,
which says: The moon
is a desiccated sun!

World, lost and forgotten
in words a thousand and one —
CHERRYTREE! while the cherrytree flowers
FLOOD! while the sea retreats
on the tracks of the moon —

it is time to stop it
and bring the world home into words,
inhabitable
dream, entrusted to breath, even in sleep
silence reached
along the graveyard lane of language,

Time, to give
cherries to summer, azure
and to let the sea roll over us,
a strong rain

Time, to be silent,
to be, among the things, wordless,
listen, when the world comes near to our house, at night
with the stepping of armadillos,
untranslatable.

C. Menkel g   7. 1965   Luft-Tier   2/2

From 'Manifesto of the Dead'

1

Anyone travelling to the realm of the dead will find, at the end of all surveyable roads, a great triumphal arch. This usually arouses pleasant sensations, and one immediately thinks of receptions, speeches, ceremonies. But the arch functions as a substitute for all those things; it is a fake signboard, erected out of a groundless sense of obligation, advertising the zone of the dead. Anyone who takes the time to look at it closer will find that it is completely decrepit, a rotting piece of architecture draped with faded flowers and fake heroes.

3

Balustrades!
Big curving parapets allowing the dead to view and survey the business of the world. While various groups of the dead bustle about in vague hinterlands, others walk up to the balustrade and engross themselves in the astounding panorama presented to their eyes by the earth's globe and all that happens on it. If the dead were spared this sight, they would, one might say, be better off. They would not need to keep making comparisons between the amplitude of the visible world and the emptiness of the zone where they reside. This comparison is certainly an annihilating one for such of them as cannot do without the sight of earth.

4

The mapmakers of the realm of the dead — they want finally to be certain of something — differ surprisingly in their opinions. There are some who make out that the frontier is a mountain range, others that it is an ocean, and others who think that the realm is round. They simply cannot agree. So they disperse, rush away in swarms, scatter far and wide into the desert, and go off in search. They make swimming motions, in order to ascertain, perhaps, that there is water, perhaps in order to be raised up and carried along by a wave; they frantically hope that they will stumble and fall, for this would mean that stones were there, which might indicate the existence of a mountain. But eventually they move forward in their usual way, completely content in their conviction that the frontiers must be sought farther off.

Those who believe that the realm is round stay behind in an enviable state of inertia. Sometimes a group of mountain-seekers will cross their horizon; their hurry tells that they still have not found the hoped-for frontiers. Or the ocean-seekers appear, quivering with zeal, traversing the void in an insistent hurry. A thousand questions. The immense inquisitiveness of the inert. And, disavowing any weakness, busily waving, the others reply: We have found traces, indications, hints! Just a little more patience!

5

It is not true that the dead can always move about freely as they choose. For the winds blow. Probably — but who can tell — they are private enterprise winds, curlicue snippets of earthly hurricanes, stray gales and waftings without fixed abode. Nevertheless, they have set up their starting lines and racetracks in the territories of the dead also. O these accursed winds!

If a squall comes, one of those unoccupied rising winds which, nobody knows why, are up and doing here, then: Watch out, take cover, quick, quick, get out of the way, it's everyone for himself.

The dead immediately rush out, run and stumble and dash across the empty terrains. Get away, and fast, get away, unless you want to get caught.

The ones who were able to escape from the wind can afford to laugh. But terror speaks in the gestures of the less mobile groups who have been caught. The strong current of air has caught them, and now it drags them along, whole legions of the dead, trembling, howling and writhing, protesting appendages of the gale, powerless, trapped.

It often happens that entire legions of the dead move into a wind shadow and are dumped there. They sit around and

wait for new tempests that might grab them up and blow them back. But then such tempests do not come. Yet, uncertain as to whether they should decide to migrate out of the wind shadow, they hang around in the hope that the return wind might come back after all to carry them home, home —
O these wretched, these underhanded, these accursed winds!

10

Shining cities have been founded, modelled on cities like New York or Venice, but they have immediately been forgotten. Their city planning stops at the founding stage. Indeed, where would the dead get the materials, money for cement and metals, and stone for even quite a small place. Sometimes, when their ideas crystallize, in moments of infinite agreement, they seem to be able to manage the top end of a modest alleyway, but no, nothing comes of it. And once the ceremonies are over they switch *en masse* to other sites, and start anew to found another colossal city, with other names, ocean bays, cathedrals, and boulevards.

Often they found cities where three others have already been founded. They revel in names and architectural forms, and they proclaim new styles. Doubtless they will found many more new cities, radiant metropolises with surprising architecture and resounding names, with spiralling snailshell apartment houses and pyramids made of fishbones, with avian monuments of flying roofs, beggars' palaces and taverns for kings and their domestics, with rivers of gold flowing over bridges of copper, and with towering dams to keep out the wind, as aforesaid —

All this, only to forget it again immediately.

14

Whenever the dead have a particular idea — and it can be said that their ideas come thick and fast and jumbled — then they leap into activity. It takes only a trivial idea to upset the dead and make them incurably agitated.

At the moment their idea is distributing pamphlets. To this end they intend to write texts, protests, suggestions, demands to be laid before those who are responsible for conditions among the dead. But where is the paper to come from, what pens will they use, in what language can one make oneself understood? They have nothing suitable. Nothing, absolutely nothing; the same old story — again and again they've heard that and forgotten it. Yet they still think that everything might change, all of a sudden.

They'll have to try other methods.

But there are none, not for them. So they absently toss aside their theoretical pamphlets, confident that their desires will be self-realizing, though they are not.

Now they are obliged to change the methods by which they have ideas.

A theoretical wind will toss the theoretical pamphlets into a megalopolis fabricated out of countless bright ideas. They must be due to arrive soon, for one can already see various groups impatiently walking back and forth and keeping watch. Eventually they stoop, gathering and collecting something, running about, sorting, folding, reading, packaging, and carrying off — the pamphlets which, it seems, have arrived in large quantities.

While the pamphlets are raining down, they suddenly have the idea that what they are holding in their hands are foreign pamphlets, with unknown texts. This makes them still more excited. They pounce on the unexpected reading material and tear the pages from one another's hands. Anyone seeing them standing around in their big crowds would conclude that incredible, unthinkable things have been happening, here and elsewhere.

16

The thought of riding on a merry-go-round has caused crowds of the dead to whirl around in the air, making circles. A pushing and spinning of numberless dead, who at the moment believe they are riding on the wooden elephants and horses of a merry-go-round.

Others, unaffected by the idea, gape at these interminable goings-on. It is a quite particularly strange occurrence for those who believe they are now at rest and are thus keeping as motionless as possible. Angels arriving on the scene have even less understanding of the merry-go-round idea. They see whirlwinds in which the poor fellows have been caught up, and off they run, to try to stop it somehow.

But regardless of their surroundings and self-obliviously the dead accelerate their merry-go-round until it reaches a pitch of ecstasy. Those who are standing outside await the moment when things will slacken and fall apart, as they must. Then those that fall will be caught, pacified, as they sober up, comfort will be given, explanations, promises, and new ideas allowed to flourish.

30

Not a one among the dead has escaped the fever of rebellious flight. New groups keep leaving, spearheads and rearguards following one another in close succession. The entire dead are on the move, singing carmagnoles.

But all at once a wind rises and blows against the hurrying throng. At first hardly any notice is taken of it, and even when it starts to blow more cold and strong, they keep courageously right on, for it is still possible to move against it.

Yet gradually the wind's roaring front hardens. Despite increasing danger the columns of the dead are filled with boundless enthusiasm. The wind is the defender of the exits, they shout, we are on the right road! But more and more it blows, a tempest now. They have to strain their utmost to press on against it. They keep closing ranks and forming bigger, denser throngs. Those who walked alone, as well as small groups, have already been extirpated, dispersed.

The going becomes more and more difficult.

Now every step is a struggle. An icy paralysing flow of wind streams and swells around the obstinate dead, resisting as they can, and no further advances are possible. Now it is only a question of holding firm to the positions gained. Sharper and colder the wind blows, as it flows against them; dispirited groups break away and let themselves be flung back. But an élite group still contrives to keep going and resists the hurricane.

Eventually their last strength is gone. The sharp cutting windflow rips the groups apart and hurls the last of the brave in somersaults and avalanches back upon their empty terrains.

Perhaps, as rumour has it, single groups have fought their way through; or a few crawling angels managed

to subvert the hurricane and penetrate into another sphere —
   But nothing is known on the subject.

Ucht

From time to time Ucht tries his hand at magic.

Whenever he gets an idea, and Ucht has them all the time, he becomes at once its advocate and builder. He does all he can to get it into some appropriate and significant form, enabling it to be independent and to live wherever it wants without further fuss on his part. Ideas are not always a joy for Ucht. They often crowd him, fifteen, twenty ideas at a time with their extraordinary demands, all in a hurry, ready to wheel around and jump at him out of the dark in a rage if he does not drop everything else on their account. That has caused Ucht a lot of trouble. For the most part he finishes with them, if only to be rid of the squirmy, impatient, presumptuous little beggars.

Many ideas do toddle off as soon as they are fitted out with a shape and some powers of their own, leaving as snow kings, snail herders, or whatever they have turned out to be, going their own ways, and Ucht loses track of them and forgets. But there are the others! For days, for nights at a time, they will rustle and rattle around his house. Birds, for example, fly against his windows, squawking with rage, convinced that Ucht has left something unfinished with a wing, a claw, or neck feathers.

What can he do but take a particular version he had thought was finished, check it over again, remodel it, and throw it out the window, certain there is nothing more he can do.

That is all very difficult for Ucht, too difficult, almost.

All those houses that he has produced in the course of time, he should arrange them better, grouping them into villages instead of letting them be swallowed up by open country. He ought to give them hope with a few hotels and shops, ensuring some character with a park or a plan. All of those fish that he has invented merely because he had the notion,

DĂ

he ought to have started out by putting them in a single school. He should have begun in a small way with one kind, so that he would be able to say, 'That's my variety, yes indeed, I can swear to it, I'd know them anywhere.' But he has dozens of fish, some here, some there, dawdling about in all sorts of water. It is enough to make you lose perspective, if not your head.

Ucht has lost contact with his creatures. When he is out and about, it can happen that he passes through settlements where his creations have tried to find some cover. They just let Ucht go right on by without a word, giving little signals to neighbours across the fence. And behind his back Ucht can hear, 'There he is, just look at him, he's the one . . .'

Naturally Ucht has grown more insecure. Everything he encounters seems to blame him. Even things he has not created take advantage of the situation, gleefully pinning it all on him, smugly getting in his way at every turn. All the shadows and figures, those partial, nameless, uncertain, untried shapes clutch at him and cover him with accusation and ridicule. And only to have some way to shift the blame of their rancour and rage from their own souls. Only to have a place of their own that Ucht cannot embody for them. Only to be able to join in some grievance that would shift the responsibility of their own helplessness. Only because they need some fall guy, some stooge.

It has cost him many bitter hours.

Then one night there is a knock at Ucht's door, and a man is standing out in the rain, and he says, 'You, Ucht? There's this dolphin fooling around out on the coast who'd like to talk to you. He's waiting for you, impatiently. Okay? Right there on the coast.'

Yes, that's so, says Ucht, and thanks a lot, and gives the man some loose change for his trouble, closing the door behind him, his heart pounding. In a rush Ucht pulls out his lists, but they are sketchy, incomplete, and he cannot find the faintest trace of a dolphin. The thought that this might be a dolphin he has made upsets him, makes his blood run cold.

He'll sit right down, make a bird, no, a goat, uh-uh a cat . . .

No, something else.

He will get right on it, invent a dog and finish it tonight. He

has had a lot of practice with dogs. He could probably give
him an owl, Ucht knows owls inside and out, but a dog will
do for now. Yes, a dog. The dolphin will take that as a sign of
goodwill.

So, a dog . . .

But will they ever meet, could they understand one
another in their different languages, especially there on the
coast, with the roaring, crashing sounds of the sea. Ucht does
not know, does not want to know. A dog . . . that's that.
Really, he is so tired. They ought to play the dolphin some
music, that would make him happy, put him in a good mood.
Dolphins love music, but they hear so little of it. Once in a
while a few measures might fall overboard from the dance
band on some cruise ship, or they might snap up a snatch or
two of a tune, a poorly played rendition of bad music, that is
little more than nothing at all.

And when he stops to think about it . . .

No, enough of that. Ucht is going to the coast. He will clear
up everything, right away. Any minute he will throw on his
raincoat and start off. He will race through the sand, calling
until he has found that dolphin. He'll set everything straight.
Any minute now . . .

Inventions

Do not suppose for a minute that fiction the way I do it is a simple diversion. As little as whaling or planting crops. My inventions do not rely on any of the usual tricks and do not take advantage of people's gullibility or their lack of imagination. There is rarely a specific purpose in mind, either to insult or to disarm. My creations are aimed at no one, they are not assaults. Whoever envies me may feel insulted, but I can only add that being able to make things up is not enviable.

If I believe it would be of advantage here and now to have a band march through the beach resort, what is to keep me from it. But I would need impeccable reasons. Let us say the mayor has died, or some foreign lady, reeking of money and possessions, has just drowned unexpectedly in the sea — then I have my grounds. The first row of drummers is just itching to step off.

Of course there are many who can invent and cast their spells without a second thought. Virtuosi, all of them, able to rely on vast repertories of ideas. As a rule they are enormously productive, they can climb any mountain four times over, and change freighters into submarines, and when the going gets rough, submarines back to freighters. They can captivate their guests by pulling islands out of inlets, village ponds, or puddles, and everything they do, in jest or boredom, comes off without a hitch. But with me, nothing ever comes of boredom.

When I am bored, I can work as long and hard as I like for some company, nothing happens. Not even a calling card.

Here is the thing with the rabbit. I could produce a rabbit, a respectable, nearly perfect rabbit. I know all the features. But what are rabbits to me. Personally I would rather have an elephant.

I could fabricate a donkey. But where from there. He

would not have a purpose, he would be doomed to a miserable pointless life, probably starving or being beaten to death. And I would have to be travelling somewhere south to do him justice. That is why I prefer to leave him alone.

Prospect

A short time ago in a whimsical mood, I printed the prospectus of a country that I had invented, one that is not on any map, although in some respects it does resemble Tibet. I circulated the brochure and was flooded immediately with correspondence and queries. Some people wanted to spend vacations there and wrote for information on hotel prices and resorts. Some wanted to emigrate, and they were interested in airline connections, ship passage, furniture movers, and job opportunities. Botanists and students of art history, nosing out new territory, wrote with academic questions. And others requested information about the language and the climate, wished for details of financial conditions and asked specific questions about casinos, sanatoriums, room and board, and various amusements.

I have wrapped myself in silence. Where am I to lodge my piece of world? The continents are full, even the islands are sold out. My only answer is to publish photographs, some vague, unfamiliar Asian scenes, that will be so appealing that the desire for my country will grow and grow.

Tower Theatre

There are, of course, public and private theatres, basement stages, cabarets in lofts, studios and outdoor theatres; and there are theatrical salons and audition halls, local play houses and supper shows.

But that is not enough for me. I have invented a tower theatre. Nothing suits my plans better than the spire of a Gothic cathedral.

I transform the ninety-metre-high octagon into an arena-like theatre in the round. I nail up balconies that end hanging in space beyond the tracery of the windows, buttressed on the weathered heads of apostles and trumpeting angels that stand at various heights on the outside walls.

The mere fact that a play is being given in a cathedral lures hordes of visitors. I have sent word to every provincial theatre and to the drama schools, and I welcome all hopelessly deluded, self-taught actors and desperate dabblers, carefully, tactfully casting all the roles.

On opening night my octagonal hall is packed. The balconies creak, and at first I am afraid they might collapse or that a trumpeting angel may crumble under the load. Following the first act, the players exit behind a wooden partition whose door opens into empty space.

Unsuspecting, they step through to what they suppose will be an adjoining room, and they crash immediately to the cobblestone pavement surrounding the cathedral. But I have planned ahead and made arrangements that someone down below will get them quickly out of the way. The tower bells ring out between the scenes and it is virtually impossible to hear the screams of falling actors. Then comes the second scene. Players are waiting to enter from the spiral staircase. In the first scene I have used one pasha, twelve servants, a princess, one Don Juan, and seven chamberlains; and the second act will cost me one pasha, a princess, one Don Juan, and three ministers of state. By the end of my play I have used six pashas, seven princesses, seven Don Juans, thirty chamberlains, five ladies' maids, nine ministers of state, and one troubadour, all of whom I have kept hidden in the draughty spiral stairway until their cues.

The applause breaks with the intensity of a hurricane, but I am worried. I cannot possibly come up with enough actors for a repeat performance. And I leave town the same night, regretting again the death of so many players.

But they have their scene, those who probably would not have had the chance otherwise.

Isn't that obvious!

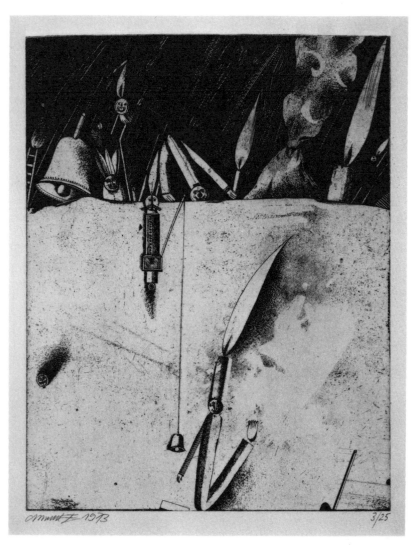

Tear Animals

(fragment of a letter)

'. . . and we haven't seen them for weeks. They left as they had come, without a trace.

'We first noticed when the jugs that we put out for them each evening in front of our doors remained empty and dry. We thought nothing of it the first time they stayed away, or even later, since we'd been indifferent to them from the start. Nobody knows how they lived. We never saw them eat anything. They were not shy, they ran around as if they were blind or totally indifferent to us and everything about us. But how could they find where we were, unless they had some sense of smell?

'There were several dozen in our neighbourhood, but they've never been seen anywhere else. Have you ever seen any? I personally watched one of them dash across a field and crash into a tree. It backed off and stared, astonished, then tried again to run through the trunk. When it crashed a second time, it just ran off around the tree without batting an eye.

'They had three legs, two in back, one in front, and black skin sparsely covered with hair. About the size of a fox. Does that give you some idea of how they looked? On their heads, two large bumps on which their eyes sat. The tears were probably in the bumps. The tears flowed constantly, even when the animals slept. They went to sleep wherever they were, in the road or next to the tear jugs, it did not seem to matter. Suddenly they would wake up in puddles of tears, stretch, shake themselves, lick their wet hides, and move a few steps to settle back to sleep.

'First we found traces of tears in the woods. We asked ourselves who might have been carrying water, and why. There were enough ponds and streams in the forest, no one needed to bring in water. Then we saw one of them. It was running along the path, it wasn't running away, it did not move slower or faster, it did not stop and it did not look up. It ran along our path with its head close to the ground, and we stopped and stared and talked about it at length and stood before our doors in the evening and told of it and spoke of the tear animals that others in the meantime had also seen. And soon we thought nothing more of them, just as you do not think about cats all the time because some are always around. We talked about them less and less, simply because we were basically indifferent to them.

'Then one time a few approached and stood before our doors, heads down, growling a little, softly, barely audible, a nasty-sounding growl. They didn't eat anything we threw to them, and then someone came up with the idea of setting out a bucket, and that must have been it, for they all crowded around and hung their heads over the rim and filled the bucket and ran away and the tears kept coming, leaving dark spots behind them.

'You can imagine that, can't you, even if you haven't seen them? We made a kind of joke of it, putting tear jugs in front of our doors, canisters, wash tubs, troughs, pails, anything, we'd find them all full in the morning. The tear water was colourless and just like ordinary water, except it had a strange smell, not sweet, not sour. We poured it out, our animals did not drink it, we did not drink it and had no use for it. It was totally superfluous.

'They did not cry about it! They did not howl and it did not look like they were suffering. They just let the tears fall silently, probably for no special reason. Naturally we did not know if they had particular troubles that caused them to cry like that, also it was not important, since they never howled or talked or paid any attention to us. They came regularly every night and filled the containers. They seemed to appreciate it. Sometimes they would growl, although you could hardly hear it, that was all.

'Now they are gone.

'At least, our containers have been empty for weeks. We don't even put them out any more. No one has seen the animals, and we ask ourselves where they have gone and what has happened and what can happen to them.

'You are asking what else we could do. Should they be

forgotten? They lived here a while and are gone now, do you think that is reason to remember them? We have poured out the tear water, there isn't any left, we should have saved some of it, perhaps it had special properties that we did not know about. We never hunted or killed one of the animals or tried to eat them, and, in fact, it is useless to go on talking about them.

'They are gone. I do want to write it down, I'll write to you about it and let it go at that, I'll write that they were here, to you, and you can read it and keep it or throw it away. What else can anybody do in this case? Let me know if something occurs to you and if you are the least bit interested in them, even though they are not here any more . . .'

The Hotel

I spent only one night in this hotel. It stood prominently on the jetty and you could hear the sea, the remarkable harmony of its thrusts. I had paid for two nights in advance, but they refused to give my money back when I left the next day.

In this odd hotel you were expected to sleep on ladders, bent over the top rung like a hanged or dead person being packed off to a mass grave over someone's shoulder. I had just stretched out on the floor — my question whether there were any beds had brought nothing but laughter — when I was jerked to my feet by my room-mates with the advice that I'd better hang over a ladder if I did not want to die.

That night one draught of fish after another squirmed and slid over the floor, in every room, even the pantry and basement, fish as long as your arm, and sharks that slashed at anything in their way. I could not understand how my room-mates were able to sleep so soundly through it all, much less that there were people who had rented rooms for several months, and at rates that seemed incredibly high.

I felt strange. I packed at once and left early in the morning.

Baan: Description of a City

Situated at the marshy end of a saltwater gulf, Baan is a great city of gallows and hundred-armed cranes. They stand in countless groups, deeply, firmly anchored in the levelled plane that supports the city, resembling emaciated brawlers who spin and turn, lift and lower their wiry, angular arms. Every building in Baan has at least one ring of iron, concrete, or wood secured to its roof. Because of their weight and bulk, churches, opera houses, casinos, palaces, and factories have several rings. Even kennels and news-stands have them.

If a springtide is reported, or if an avalanche is seen crashing down the mountains at whose foot Baan sprawls, the arms of the cranes and gallows swiftly begin to lower and fasten their metal hooks, clamps, and anchors into the rings. The buildings, standing on the ground compact and mobile as boxes, are hoisted quickly and remain swaying and creaking in the air until all danger has passed. Arms of smaller cranes come out of the windows to snag various lighter objects, such as pigsties, lawn chairs, billboards, boat-houses, taxi cabs, each of which also is fitted with a ring.

The tide rages over empty ground. Many belongings, kennels, bicycles, water troughs, or children's wagons, may not be hooked in time, and they fall victim to the surging saltwater and are washed away. But what are those losses compared to this metropolis, swinging safely high and dry. Under the fierce blows of flood and avalanche, the cranes and gallows begin taking up slack and start to sway, and if strong wind accompanies invading water and snow, entire quarters of the city begin to gyrate and creak ominously. Buildings crunch their corners together hard enough to splinter windows and make plaster crack and crumble, but nothing more serious happens.

Many sleeping people are rolled from their beds when the houses are lifted. Tables and cabinets ram against walls.

Merkel Drama   3/5

Singers topple over at the opera houses, curtains falling in
heaps about them. After the water has run its course and the
mountain has strewn its frozen debris, the buildings are
lowered. Following an earthquake, extreme care is taken to
ensure that structures are not put down in pits or craters, or
left to stand on the rim of fissures. Slowly the city sinks and
settles into place. The bits and pieces, houses and huts, are
set down, and churches are manoeuvred carefully to hastily
consecrated ground.

Hardly a building ends up on its previous site. New
boulevards and prospects unfold and are duly inspected and
soon put to good use by the inhabitants of Baan. Neighbours
have disappeared without a trace. Luxury hotels turn up in
the slums and whole villas perch on jetties. Swiftly Baan
grows accustomed to its new character, and the cranes are
cleaned and re-oiled.

20/25

My Friends

I kept watch at the entrance of a complex labyrinthine cave that penetrated to the core of a large mountain. From a booth plastered with timetables and posters I sold scenic cards, brochures, and maps of passageways and tunnels and collected admission fees. There was little traffic in the area and I did not have much to do.

I spent years at this job and nothing worth mentioning ever happened. But one day I was shaken by an event that set my nerves on edge. Toward the end of last summer someone emerged from the cave whom I did not remember admitting. This person tipped his hat and went nonchalantly on his way. At first I thought I had made a mistake. But similar things kept happening.

Much to my amazement numerous other people followed. Several stopped to ask about train connections or to request names of inexpensive hotels in the surrounding small towns. The traffic of unfamiliar persons leaving the cave steadily increased, and I kept telling myself to be calm, not to lose my head. Sailors swaggered out, carrying parts of ships or dragging figureheads, helm wheels, tillers, or battered skiffs. Rats swarmed after them. I supposed that ships had sunk inside the mountain; no doubt there had to be subterranean seas with heavy traffic.

Stray dogs trotted down from the mountain. I stopped letting people in and began keeping track of all who left by making sketches of them. After work once I dashed through passages and caverns but could find no other entrance.

The stream of strangers was constant. Deep in conversations, these people seemed not to notice me. I rapped on the windows of my booth, demanding some explanation, but not one of them ever turned around. Chinese emerged, closing dripping umbrellas. My head was awhirl. There could be foreign nations in that mountain, tracts that had survived from fairy tales, sunken cities of bats, veritable harems of graves recently jarred by some strange resurrecting wave, penal colonies, secret societies, and uncharted lands. What did all that stuff buried in the mountain mean to me! I quit my job, packed up and left, and became a waiter in an expensive hotel in a large city.

Things went well for me at first. But after a while I began to recognize among my patrons certain people whom I had seen coming out of the cave, foreigners who sat smoking and talking around the tables in my salon. Their actions in no way indicated that they recognized me. Almost daily I discovered some new emigré from the labyrinth.

Accidents, I told myself, nothing more than comical coincidence. Why shouldn't these people live and eat here. Certainly it was their right and it might even be their usual practice. But finally I quit again; it was so uncanny. I opened a paper-bag shop in another city.

Those people were among my first customers. I grew more insecure. What did they want from me? And what in the world did they want with my paper bags? And I left again. I had to be free of it; they were getting me down, those people! I travelled over two hundred kilometres and took a job as a streetcar conductor in Constantinople. Each day my car was filled with those familiar, so familiar, so unwanted, so despised people. They held out their tickets without looking up from beneath their hats and turbans. And slowly my opinion of them began to change.

It has dawned on me that they have nothing against me. On the contrary, I think I notice that they take comfort in presence. Closeness to me seems to offer them something they may not have themselves. Often I almost feel responsible for them. If I should change jobs again, I foresee serious problems. I am afraid, as confused as they are, they would tumble head over heels trying to find me and would not have any peace until they did. If they are vampires, they certainly are not doing me any harm. If they are poor, at least they are not begging. Of course they do not show their hand, and they go on as if they did not even see me.

They might be creatures or refugees from some frag-mented tale, heroes cut off in exile, or shades who somehow have missed the boat and are trying to keep track of how I

succeed, let them be whatever they are! — they have obliged
me to live well. I have gone to great expense, rented an
apartment in a reputable hotel, I am well dressed and know
how to look busy. This way of life probably would not have
been my own choice, but I do feel at home in it. Were I to lead
a footloose existence in back alleys, draughty lofts, or chilly
basements, I would soon have a bad conscience. Perhaps
then they would leave me alone. But I do not doubt that in my
apparent good fortune, I am an encouraging sight for them.
And I do believe that I, or better, the way I am living, does
give them much to talk about and much excitement, ample
ground for speculation and racking their brains.

That is the way things stand between us. I give parties,
actually only to lure them out and to find some way of
meeting one or another of them face to face; but I have never
caught sight of any of them among my guests. Our meetings
are wordless, but our trust is lasting. If I were to speak to one
of them, expressing the wish to have supper with him, I
would have to be prepared for an indignant stare.

I often wonder if they know one another. I wonder, too, if
other people are privileged to have similar followings. I once
talked to a friend, hinting broadly about such things, but he
seems to have experienced none of this, at least he did not
appear to understand what I was getting at.

Yesterday one of them was coming toward me. He glanced
away quickly when he saw me. As I looked back at him, I
noticed that he seemed about to turn around in my direction.
For an instant I considered nodding to him. But I kept
walking.

End of the World

Legends tell of a man who will appear one day and, through the magical powers of his eyes, empty the world by looking. That is, his glance will be able to move things from their places, settling them intact behind his pupils and eyelids. This man, so it goes, exhausted by ceaseless, intensive observing, will have collected the entire world behind his eyes; and the shifted life will go on in his head, with its ebb and flow, fairs and moon phases. As itself or its own memory? Caricature or intricate echo?

And the man will absorb all sounds, speech, and music and will breathe all smells. In the end nothing will be left but him, covering and store of an inexhaustible world that can never die.

Railroads and bird flights whose paths cross over behind his eyes will keep watch through his pupils and eyelid slits for their origins and initial courses, for possible tracks and shadowy traces, but they will see as little, as astoundingly little as an insect might have seen through a porthole of Noah's ark. And if this man, aware one day of his own loneliness, tries to place something outside himself for company, a house, a dog, or a patch of flowers, his relentless, consuming gaze will anticipate the scene, restraining it even against his will, not allowing it out of his head.

His eyes, they say, will become great show windows where pieces of world celebrate their miraculous survival with cardboard houses and fragments of sky, holidays and dance halls, but no one will ever turn up who would see it all going on behind his eyelids, for they would be captured immediately by one of those glances and, however they might resist, they, too, would find themselves entering and descending through the eyes of this man into the realm of chime-playing and pear-plants inside his head.

The Lion

A lion came into my house at night and lay down beside me.
At first I did not know that it was a lion. I heard something
tapping and groping its way through my house, whose doors
were open; I saw something wide and dark coming into my
room, it snuffled at me, and lay down beside me. In the
half-light I recognized, later, a lion. He was breathing deeply
and regularly and he soon fell asleep, it seemed. From his
mane came a smell of mould and leaves, wet fresh earth and a
wild animal-smell which quite dazed me. I could tell that the
lion was wet, the moisture dripping from his skin. He spread
coolness all around him. To reach me, he must have swum
across the big river near by.

It was autumn, cool winds were crossing the plain and they
came fresh into my house that was still warm from the
summer. They came from the high plateaux, or from the sea,
and you could hear them, loud, in the night. That night I
slept well. The lion, too, seemed to sleep quietly and well;
toward morning, a warmth came from his body. In the
twilight of morning I woke; the lion had got up and was
standing in front of my house, where, when hours later I left
my room, he was still standing, looking at the big river.

I beckoned to him and fed him with meat that I had in the
house. I hoped that the lion would speak a few words to me
now, but he was obstinately silent; true, he looked at me,
from time to time, with his dark eyes, but it seemed he had
nothing to tell me. Eventually, I gave up expecting him to
speak to me. Often I talked to him in my language and I
thought he showed signs of having understood me.

During the following nights, the lion slept beside me
again. He spent the days near the house. Against the sun I
saw him standing, black, on a hill and gazing in the direction
of the sea; I saw him standing by the river and looking into
the flowing water with his head bowed down. Sometimes he

Vulkan

would trot through my house or lie in the sun against its walls, or across the threshold; he moved slowly and quietly. I went about my work as usual and met him frequently during the day.

Once, when I was about to leave the house for quite some time, I said to the lion: You must decide whether, during my absence, which may last for several days, you wish to stay inside the house or outside it, for I want to lock the door. Instead of answering, the lion lay down on the threshold, and I knew that I did not need to lock my house. I went away and knew it for certain. When I came back, during the late September rainfalls, the lion was lying open-eyed just inside the door. When he saw me, he came out of the house. In the house everything was as I had left it. I thanked the lion and put out for him some meat which I had brought with me.

The lion often sat beside me when I stood fishing by the river. He sniffed at the fish I caught and looked at me attentively. He accompanied me through the forest, when I went to cut wood (there were no lions anywhere here), and every night he slept beside me. Then the lion left me. The first snow was in the air. One morning, in the twilight, he touched me as he got up, to wake me, and he looked at me. I took this as a sign that he was leaving, accompanied him to the door of my house, saw him walk in the rain to the river, saw him swim across the river and grow smaller and vanish in the curtain of rain on the plain beyond the river.

This was the only thing which happened that year in my house by the river. I cannot remember any other events, except for those connected with my work, unimportant ones. Winter came and went. The cold hung green and rustling over the river, which was free of ice because of its strong current. The sky stood glassy clear and hung full of snow. I visited a few people near by and farther off; other people visited me in my house. During this time I did not see the lion.

In the spring I repaired the roof of my house, replaced half the roof beams with new ones, put new floorboards and flagstones down, and went about my work as usual. The log rafts drifted down the big river to the sea. I still hoped that the lion would come again to visit my house, but I did not expect that he would. At the beginning of the summer I saw a heavily cloaked man riding a donkey on the far side of the river, coming over the plain. On a long string an enormous red owl floated out in front of him, flying in circles high up in the wind. The rider was riding down the river. We shouted greetings and questions and answers across the river, but did not understand each other because of the considerable distance. It occurred to me that the rider might be somehow connected with the lion. When he had gone, I quickly forgot him. For several weeks, nothing happened; I went on doing my work. One evening in the summer there was a donkey standing on the other side of the river, holding a black fish in his mouth. Doubtless he could have caught the fish between his teeth while drinking. When the donkey saw me, he turned about with a few quick leaps and ran off across the plain. He took the fish with him in his mouth. Darkness was coming on, and I lost sight of the donkey.

Again for a long time nothing happened. The summer shone across the plain. I did my work, as usual, and had my pleasure in the warmth and the light. The windows and doors of my house stood wide open all night, so that a breeze could keep blowing through and drive away the heat which collected in the rooms during the daytime. Sometimes I thought of the lion and I thought of him with joy. But I did not see him again.

In the late summer, with the hot noon trembling over the plain, I saw the cloaked rider coming down the river near to my house. Tied to a string behind him walked the lion which had once been in my house. On the lion's back sat the enormous red owl, which was very much larger than the lion. The owl was holding the black fish in its beak. The lion seemed to be finding the owl heavy. He put his paws slowly down and walked with his head hung low. This little caravan came past very close to my house. Lion, owl and donkey looked at me, I was standing in the doorway of my house. The cloaked man turned his head and gave me a long stare with the white slits of his eyes. The lion looked at me the longest. I hoped that the group would stop at my house, perhaps to ask for some fresh water to drink, but it passed by and slowly vanished in the plain down the river. I stared after them for a long time. That day I missed doing any of my work.

I have never seen the group again. Neighbours who live miles away in the hills by the river also remembered having seen the procession that day. Nothing more happened. Sometimes I remember them; and on the days when I think of the lion, I often miss doing my usual work.

Tullipan

Suddenly one morning in spring Tullipan was standing in the doorway of my room, clearing his throat and scuffing his feet on the theshold. I was sitting at my desk and did not turn around, for I thought the shoemaker I had invited the night before had just stepped in. Or a telegram, a special delivery letter, I thought, a salesman, perhaps, or the fish peddler I was expecting that day, or the man who comes every other week to collect my empty cans and bottles; I sat at my desk, continued writing for a few seconds, then turned and, for the first time, caught sight of Tullipan.

I was no more surprised than that, grasped his form in a single glance, noticing nothing but him, this apparition of a familiar figure that, tall and broad, filled the squat door frame; I noticed no single feature, not his nose or hands, his hair, his clothes, or his shoes; I saw nothing but him at my door, and I heard his dark laughter, which was the single thing about him that I did distinguish and seize upon: *Tullipan is standing in the doorway. He is laughing.* In reality I was no more astonished than if a peddler had stopped by, or someone I knew in the neighbourhood to show me a review in the newspaper, or to ask if I would like a ride to the city, the car was right outside, or some such thing that so often happened in the morning. I pulled up a chair and said to Tullipan: 'I am in a hurry to finish some work, it won't take long. Sit down, Tullipan, wait a minute.'

But Tullipan, whose deep laughter lingered, whose laughter I marvelled at (never had I imagined his voice) and which reminded me of things past, lost, or forgotten, was in no mood to sit down. He went to the window and looked out, stared into space, and laughed under his breath. He tugged at my sleeve and glanced over my shoulder at what I had begun writing that morning. 'Yes, yes,' I said, 'I'm nearly finished, Tullipan, sit down over there and be patient.' And Tullipan sat down, dragging the chair up next to me, unlaced his shoes and threw them to the floor, groaned with relief and rubbed his toes, scratched his neck, sniffed and snorted, and wiped the sweat from his face with his fists. At last his presence disturbed me so much that I stood up from my desk.

I looked at Tullipan. I wanted nothing more than to examine him closely and calmly, this complete, huge Tullipan, inch by inch, slowly, at length. But I did not have time.

'Go on and make some coffee.' Tullipan said, laughing into my face and standing up too.

Oh, Tullipan! A difficult time began that morning. I had never reckoned that you could ever spring from my head. You were the last thing I expected.

Now, after months and years, I am setting to work, trying to give Tullipan the form which I should have given him from the start. That, I have not done, and now, since I am working with whatever powers I have, the powers of a writer who writes stories and puts together all manner of prose, who makes books and poems, poems — now, it is quite late for that, perhaps too late.

Earlier, while relaxing or exhausted, on walks, roaming about, in trains and waiting rooms, standing in line, or drunk, for my own pleasure and personal amusement, out of arrogance, perhaps, and daydreams, I had created a fantastic character, giving it the name Tullipan. Tullipan was a secret possession to be shared with nothing and no one, not a soul, not a single word, not one drop of ink or piece of paper. Tullipan was a pure and magnificent luxury that entertained and entranced me whenever I wished. Tullipan increased my sense of myself and enriched and heightened my awareness. He had taken shape slowly over a period of years, and only following countless changes did I give him his name. Tullipan was a challenge without risk, a game without rules or end. Using him I explored the uncertain, unproven powers of my fantasy. And I love him in his exclusive dependence on me and my will. Tullipan signified riches and uninterrupted dreams. Tullipan was whatever came easily to me. And I feared losing this treasure if I, caught up in my profession, were someday to begin embodying Tullipan in words and sentences. Then, I felt, his magic and my wealth would be lost. Tullipan, in the form of some casual short story, would slip away and because I wanted to keep him in my imagination, I did not make a project or task of him. I wanted to be certain of him in a special and easy way.

But Tullipan got ahead of me. He has taken me by surprise and sent my beautiful dream flying. Most likely he has not been happy with me, he did not want to go on indefinitely being a shadow, invisibly existing in a beautiful, but unreal, world. Since he was there in my head, complete and ready for life, he wanted to be more than a man's dream or his toy puppet. He wanted to assert his right to be seen, he wanted — yet, I do not know what Tullipan wanted. He wanted to live and at last be among people, yes, and maybe it was just a trick he wanted to play, getting the notion into his head simply to appear before me when it suited him. One spring morning at the door of my room. 'Here I am, Tullipan,' he meant to say, 'are you glad? Do you know me? How do you feel about all this? To bewilder, harass, disturb, leave me doubting my sanity, and really put me to shame, he wanted perhaps — no, no. Tullipan did not want that. He merely did not want to miss the chance of coming just once into the world, that, above all, he wanted for himself, before I, becoming preoccupied with something else perhaps, could have left him unfinished, or could have disowned him, forgotten him, scuttled him along with irrelevant and futile things, shaking my head and only a trifle bemused —

And he has done just that. He has taken things into his own hands. He has stepped into the light of the world and into my house, put me in the wrong, taught me a lesson, and left me in the lurch.

That was some time ago. Now I am able to consider with a clear head what then cost me my peace and quiet. And now, sitting behind the typewriter in my house by the sea, I am attempting to make up for what I should have been doing from the start: using my powers to help Tullipan gain a human, visible shape, letting go of those comfortably carefree, god-like reveries, and taking upon myself the strains and burden of creating him word by word and line by line, sentence by sentence, chapter by chapter, which, as I see it now, would have been much less time-consuming and exhausting then than was his sudden appearance in my house and everything that followed. Now, I am trying to make up for all of that and am having great difficulty. At this point I cannot just sit down and write a piece of prose about Tullipan, defining my attitudes and impressions of him as I might with a casual bit of ready material. How, I am asking now, is the Tullipan of my dreams to be brought into accord with the living Tullipan? Are they identical? Will I yield perhaps to a fantastic figure because I now know the real Tullipan, slighting him in favour of some shape that enjoys the advantage of having never suddenly emerged, caught me by surprise, or caused any trouble? Who is Tullipan? How can I once more come to know the essential features of my creation?

I must rely on what I have, the skills of my profession, and have to evoke Tullipan myself, line by line. As best I can, I have to pick up his trail anew, and the reward for this work — it weighs on me like a gigantic mound of rubble on a buried badger that can scarcely breathe and for as long as it takes must try to work free if it wants to survive — yes, the reward for my effort would be the enormous and incomparable satisfaction of finally having done justice to my creation, of having made him live, unique and complete in words through those means on which I must rely, which I am forced to use and thrust, whether I like it and succeed or not. And my reward would be in being able to say: there is nothing more to be done here. It is finished and I can begin something new. *Tullipan is now as he should have been from the beginning.*

Here and now I have to sit down and sketch, make notes, remember, compare, probe, collect and edit, revise, and write, write, write . . .

Since he depended solely on my will, the Tullipan of my dreams and imaginings was an ideal and perfect creature. I could treat him as I wished and did not need to justify my conduct. I sent him forth and fetched him back as I pleased. I had him moving through mountains, salt marshes, bogs, cities, villages, invented landscapes and dreamed-up valleys, in war, catastrophe, defeat, Tullipan was my hero and my champion, I dressed him according to whimsy or need, as king or cowboy, vagabond, clown, and dandy, as a favourite son or convict, a tramp or man about town. As far as I was concerned, he could eat thistles and camp in swamps or on snake-infested islands and never needed to become sick or to die because of it.

Tullipan had to fulfil all of my fancies. Because I loved him, he was a lovable creature, and for the most part I put him in favourable and pleasant situations whenever I had him in mind. I imagined that he delighted, enchanted, captivated the people he met, I enjoyed seeing him dance at fancy balls, where he wore a white dinner jacket, I pictured him on the arms of beautiful women, and even though he was odd and never dressed in the latest style and was usually run down at the heels, they loved, honoured, seduced him, perhaps admiring and pampering him at the same time. Tullipan might be tired and worn out, half-dead and ill-tempered, sick, downtrodden, even repulsive, but he was never deceitful and no one ever doubted him. And even then I was never very clear in my own mind whether he might not be assuming aspects of a dream image of myself that had to challenge him and alter his own essential identity. I was never able to determine whether I kept him alive in my head for his sake or for my own, and even before that question would have been settled, to his disadvantage, perhaps, or to mine, he had abruptly taken things into his own hands, had pushed everything else casually aside, and, as if by chance, had walked in through my door.

One spring morning Tullipan suddenly appears and asks me to make him some coffee, he is cold. It is still early and I have not been at my desk very long. It is a gloomy day, and sharp, cold gusts of wind are blowing from the sea. I have closed the window, a fire has been roaring and crackling for half an hour and the room is just beginning to warm. Before going to the kitchen, I look at Tullipan. (The terror caused by having my own creation call on me in person overwhelms me later when I have had time to think.) He is wearing an old faded blue uniform coat and yellow rumpled wide-cuffed trousers. His black hair has been mussed by the wind. His hands and feet are large, his ponderous body towers over me by half a head.

Tullipan, too, is looking at me with curiosity, but without any trace of uneasiness. (He was flatly disconcerting, of course, and that pleased me, but repelled me at the same time, at least at first, for until that moment I had always looked on Tullipan as being totally dependent on my own will. And so, had it still been left to me, he could have been, as I was thinking at the time, a little more reserved, and a hint of nervousness would have suited him nicely.) He looks straight into my eyes and seems to notice nothing else. Since we cannot continue to stare into each other's eyes, I hurry off to the kitchen to make some coffee.

We talk through the open doors. Tullipan has taken a cigarette from my desk and is lying on the sofa, waiting for his coffee.

'Surely you're freezing,' I say, 'your clothes are wet, you ought to dry them. You can hang them on the back of the chair and move it up to the fire. I'll bring you something dry to put on in a minute.'

'No need, now,' calls Tullipan, 'froze a bit outside, you know, but I'm not out there now.'

'Where are you from?' I ask while getting out the sugar, coffee pot, and cups.

'From down there,' he says, and I cannot see if he is motioning with his hands. I put the water on the burner and grind coffee through the small, clattering mill.

'Do you always work this time of day,' asks Tullipan's sombre voice, ringing slowly through the room, 'or what are you doing . . .?'

'Yes, I work nearly every morning at this time,' I say, 'and I work until three o'clock or so.'

'And then what do you do?'

'What do I do then? I don't do a thing. Then I go down to the sea or up to the river, sometimes to the mouth, it's only half an hour away, or I go to town, a bus comes right by here, sometimes I even take my bicycle. Or I sleep for an hour or repair my bicycle, or take care of my mail, or read, or people stop to visit and I drink tea or wine with them, and we talk . . .'

'It's always like that?' asks Tullipan. He is coughing, he has swallowed some smoke.

'It isn't always just like that,' I say, 'but even if it were, it

really would not make much difference to me. I might even
like it. I travel much. I travel for six months at a time, moving
around, and no one really knows where I am. In fact it is not
possible to say exactly what I usually do, for I do not do
anything regularly, except for my work. And I am apt to do
things that five minutes earlier I did not want to do at all,
things that had not occurred to me then.'

While I am talking, I carry the coffee into the room.
Tullipan is lying on the sofa, dangling his arms.

'AHH,' he calls out when he sees me, 'I brought something
for you, too! Wait!' He springs from the sofa, runs barefoot
to the door, and returns with a large, shabby, battered
suitcase. He puts it on the table and opens it. With both
hands he removes a large round white stone and holds it out
to me.

I take the stone and lay it on the floor. 'It's so beautiful,' I
say, 'a beautiful stone, I like it. You brought it just for me?'

Tullipan nods, pushing the suitcase down from the table,
and comes over beside me and looks at the white stone from
my angle.

'You're chilled to the bone,' I say, 'you must drink some
coffee.' Tullipan climbs on to the sofa again, and I pour him a
mug of coffee, he stirs in five heaped spoonfuls of sugar. Both
of us drink steaming coffee.

'Are you hungry,' I ask.

'Oh yes, you know,' says Tullipan, the cup in both hands
close to his mouth, 'it would be terrific to have something to
eat, too!'

'Good,' I answer, 'I'll dash out and pick up some things. I
don't have much in the house. Wait just a minute!'

'Okay,' rumbles Tullipan, pouring coffee and sugar into
his huge cup. I take my bicycle off the porch and ride the five
minutes down the stretch of sandy path to the little store on
Meerstrasse, a shack made of wood and tin beneath eternally
leafless, parched, and twisted trees, and hastily buy two full
sacks of groceries: eggs and ham, herring, mustard, cheese,
olives, butter and cans of stew, schnaps and red wine,
potatoes, chocolate and sausage.

'You know, I have company this morning,' I explain to the
old woman in the shop. She nods cautiously and is attentive
and polite, for I am the only customer.

And I ride back and carry the bags to the kitchen and
return to my room where Tullipan was sitting when I left, but
he is nowhere to be found. The sofa is empty, the cup
drained.

'Tullipan,' I call, 'here are good things, come and eat
something!' And straightway out of my bedroom slowly and
proudly down the stairs comes Tullipan and halts squarely
before me, laughing and flashing meaningful looks. I have
difficulty recognizing him. He has stretched my old blue
striped bathrobe across his back, it reaches above his knees
and is much too tight through the shoulders. On his head at
an angle sits a tall, black hat, the one I had found and left in a
closet when I moved in. A pair of bright khaki trousers
extends below the robe, and on his feet I see tennis shoes with
untied, mud-trampled laces, and I do not know whether
Tullipan had them on when he first appeared or has just
found them.

'Ho, Tullipan,' I say, 'you are all dressed up?'

'Found them all right here, you know,' he says and looks
himself over, 'so, I've made myself like new; it's better this
way. You've got plenty of things, big closets just stuffed full!'

And I recall that Tullipan is hungry, push him along into
my study, and lay out on the table all of the things I have
brought. Tullipan moans with anticipation when he sees the
numerous cartons and cans. He follows me into the kitchen
and watches everything I do, carries forks and knives, plates
and glasses back to the room and sets them out on the table.
We sit down and begin eating, Tullipan works with both
hands, gulping and gasping with pleasure between huge
bites. The bathrobe gets in his way, he throws it off, the
easier to move his arms while cutting bread and ham and to
pull dishes and bottles closer. He keeps the tall hat on his
head. 'Good meal,' he says with his mouth full, 'tastes good,
you know. Where'd you get all this stuff?'

'I got it at the store on Meerstrasse,' I say, 'I do all my
shopping there.'

'In the store on Meerstrasse,' he says, 'all this?'

'Yes, and there is much, much more,' I answer. 'There is
everything you would ever want. Treasures fit for a king.
There are sausages and chocolate walruses, and buckets,
fly-traps, porcelain ships, cocoa, pillow feathers, knives and

shovels and stockings and green ink and red, old sailor pictures with ghostships and hand-written dedications, and lampshades, lottery tickets, tea-kettles . . .'

'Ahhh,' says Tullipan, 'I've got to go.' He puts his knife and fork on the table and starts to get up from the sofa.

'But not now,' I say, 'finish your meal first.'

That makes sense to him and we finished eating. Then we drink more coffee, along with some schnaps, light our cigars and relax.

Then Tullipan insists on going to the store. 'Got to get out,' he says, 'I'm full up to here, want to look around, you see.' And he braces his arms against the back of the sofa and tries to push himself up, but falls back, breathing heavily.

'You are tired, Tullipan,' I say, 'you ought to rest, you can go down to Meerstrasse anytime you want.'

'Tired, hmmm,' Tullipan says loudly, 'I'm not tired,' He laughs. 'Me, tired? not one bit.' And he lifts himself heavily from the sofa, bumps back the table, and starts for the door.

'But you can't go out like that,' I call after him, 'wait, listen, Tullipan!'

'You're right,' he says, wheeling around, and pulls the bathrobe from the arm of the sofa, squeezes himself into it, knots the belt across his belly, waves and laughs and goes out the door. I can hear him running down the hall across the front yard; heavy steps.

Once I was alone in the house, it became clear to me that the new arrival was Tullipan, my own creation, he had actually called on me. Terror shot through my bones with such force that I ran about in the house, stunned and confused, stood idly around, stared out the window, and pondered what was to happen next.

(Neighbours told me a few days later that Tullipan, suitcase in hand, had come along the beach from the south and had gone straight away to my door. Apparently he had asked no one for directions.)

I was alone until late afternoon. Tullipan did not come back. I had been waiting long enough, had tried to work, and even done some reading, and when he still had not returned after an additional half-hour that I spent doing nothing, I left the house to look for him.

I walk directly to the store and ask the old woman whether Tullipan has been in. 'My visitor,' I say.

'You mean that big . . . somebody so . . . how to put it . . . ?'

'Yes,' I say, 'that is the one, then he has been here?'

'He was in a few hours ago,' said the old woman and looks at me reproachfully.

'Good, then I'll still be able to find him,' I say.

'Is that . . . your visitor?' the old woman asks.

'Yes, yes, my guest,' I say, somewhat confused, and leave. I race down the beach to the north, turn back after half an hour, pass again through the village and move off to the south on the beach along the highway, and in the twilight, when I have nearly lost patience, I see him, Tullipan, hat on his head, in the bathrobe, standing up to his knees in seawater. He has his elbows tucked into his sides and is staring down into the shallow, sandy foam which lightly swirls around his legs.

'Haalllooo, Tullipan!' I call, 'what's the matter, why don't you come home?'

He turns and, in spite of the twilight, recognizes me at once, waves wildly, joyfully with both arms, slowly backs out of the water, then pivots and runs as fast as he can across the beach toward me, lumbering heavily through the dark, yielding sand, his hair flying in tangles, the bathrobe fluttering. He jolts to a stop next to me, breathless, he is soaked from head to toe, the pockets of the robe are crammed and bulging, his laughter comes quickly and hoarsely from his open mouth.

'There you are,' he shouts, 'look!'

Leaning at an angle, in a ceremony of cocked elbows and dripping fingers, he digs some stones out of his pockets, a fish head, a rusty knife blade, an onion-shaped piece of cork, a small, battered tin box.

'There,' he says, 'found them for you, go on, take them!'

'Thank you, Tullipan,' I say 'that is so nice of you, I am delighted. But now let's go back home.'

'Oh yes,' he says, 'you know, you can give me a bed to sleep in, where I can lie down, will you give me one?'

'Oh, you'll have a bed,' I say, wondering where I can put him up. Tullipan is wet and tired. His trousers cling dark and twisted to his legs. The sleeves of the bathrobe are dripping, his tennis shoes squeak with water. He carefully watches what I do with his gifts. I put them into my coat pockets. A long, satisfied laugh moves across his face.

Tiredly we walk home through the village. It has grown dark and Meerstrasse is veiled with deep greys. High-moving clouds above the sea reflect the last, fleeting golden light. The background of the sea stretches out grey and flat like a sheet of tin. Dark swells and waves shape streaks of foam, tugging and beating dully against the shore. Tullipan struggles along next to me, muttering to himself.

'Ohhh,' he says, 'I think I'm tired now, dog-tired, you know, um-hmmm!' Tullipan sighs and tugs at his wet clothing.

'You can go right to bed,' I say, 'and sleep as long as you want. You'll have a large mattress, it will be so comfortable.'

'Um-hmmm,' Tullipan whispers, 'that's so nice, can use it, you know, umm-hmmm . . .'

Tullipan spends the night wrapped in covers in a large old bed that I have moved from the attic to a room on the top floor. In the morning he wakes me up. It is already ten o'clock, during the night the fire has gone out, the house is filled with biting cold, and the windows are clouded with moisture. Pale sunlight filters into the bedroom. Tullipan comes to my bed, he has the tall hat on his head and holds a lighted cigar. He is wearing a pair of straw sandals I did not notice the day before.

'You know what makes me wonder,' he says and sits down on the edge of the bed. I look at him quizzically.

'That shop on Meerstrasse, you know, really makes me wonder. I was just down there and got a pile of things together, but somebody, a woman, rather fat, I think, she told me I couldn't take the things, I'm supposed to leave them there, it just wouldn't do. And I had a lot of stuff besides things to eat, too bad!'

'Look,' I say, 'that's understandable. In a store you can't put things in a sack and leave with whatever you like. First, you must . . .'

'I already thought of that,' says Tullipan, 'that's what I was thinking. If I hang around more, then I'll get the stuff all right. I've just got to be around longer, yes, maybe a few days, the woman has to keep seeing that it is me, you mean, and maybe she has to know I belong here and I'm living with you, have my own bed and everything, then she'll know the score and give me things. Yes, I was thinking that myself when she took back all my things. I was thinking just that.'

'Listen to me, Tullipan,' I say, 'you see, it's this way: when you go to any store, you need . . .'

But Tullipan has already stood up, and is leaving the room, blowing a trail of smoke, paying no attention to me, and I hear him walking in front of the house, whistling and talking to himself.

'Where did you get those straw sandals?' I ask as we are eating breakfast later in the warm study.

'Found them,' says Tullipan.

'I didn't know I had anything like that in the house,' I say, 'I had completely forgotten.'

'Not here,' says Tullipan with a meaningful look. 'Somewhere else,' he says, studying the food on his fork.

I ask him where he has found the sandals.

'Oh, you know, in a different house, not this one,' he says.

'So, in another house,' I say, 'someone gave you a present, or did you just walk in and pick them up?'

'Over there,' he says, motioning vaguely with his butterbright knife in the direction of the front door. 'I found them there. They were lying on this little chest.'

'Tullipan,' I say firmly, 'you will take the sandals back. You have to return them, do you understand?'

He laughs a little uncertainly. 'But I like them,' he says.

'That has nothing to do with it,' I say. 'You must put the sandals back on the chest, today.'

'Can I do it later,' says Tullipan, 'when I don't like them any more? I still like them, would like to use them a little, you know.'

'But you cannot go off somewhere, jerk open a door, and carry away what you like,' I say, 'or just walk into a house where people are sitting down to supper and say: Excuse me please, what you have on the stove really looks good, smells wonderful, I'd probably like it, I'll just take some with me. Can you do that?'

'I don't know,' answers Tullipan, 'never did it, but I could. And what about you? I'm getting fed here, yesterday I ate my fill, and now I think I'll be full again. Half-filled now, you know. Things taste good here.'

'But the straw sandals,' I say, 'just think of the sandals.' Tullipan is chewing and looks at me thoughtfully. 'I've got them on my feet,' he says, 'I am thinking about them, of course. When I put them on or take them off, and when they make me nice and warm I am thinking of them, believe me.'

We continue eating.

'Did anyone see you wearing the sandals?' I ask.

Tullipan ponders with his head to one side. 'I think so, there on the path as I was on my way afterwards,' he says, 'a man. He stopped in his tracks when he saw me. I stopped too, and we talked, said a few words.'

'Did he notice the straw sandals, the ones you are wearing?' I ask.

'These?' says Tullipan. 'Oh, I don't know. He did look at them, maybe they did strike him. He looked at my hat for a long time, and my coat, too, really gave me the once over, and I think it caught his eye, even at quite a distance, as I saw it, that someone was coming. Right beneath his nose such a beard he had, full of black hairs hanging out every which way, and he was pulling a wagon with a stick, full of bricks and a broom and other things. Caught my eye. Why don't you ever ask what catches my eye?'

'All right, Tullipan,' I ask, 'what did you notice in addition to the sandals?'

'The sea,' says Tullipan, 'the sea caught my eye. Even yesterday, and this morning, too, when I was out and saw it. You were still asleep, sound asleep with your eyes closed tight. It always catches my eye when I look at it, the sea. It's beautiful. And so large. At first, I believed it was only collected rainwater. But that's not it. It does not come from the rain. You have a nice house because it is so close by. Did you find it because it's so close to the sea?'

'That was one of the reasons why I moved in,' I say.

'And why else?' asks Tullipan.

'I like the entire area,' I say. 'I like the plains and the mountains beyond, and the river. The longer I am here, the better I like it, and right now I do not know if I'll ever leave.'

'And me, will I like it better and better, too,' asks Tullipan, 'later, when I am here longer, even better than now?'

'That may well happen,' I answer, 'one thing after another will catch your eye, then hardly anything will, at least not as sharply, and then it will all be a part of you. It will belong to you and you will like it.'

'Yes, I believe that,' says Tullipan, 'I believed that the first time I saw your house and the sea behind it, the sea . . .'

From that day forth I knew that Tullipan would be staying with me. As much as I dreaded the interruptions his presence would cause (and at that time I wanted nothing more than peace and quiet for my work; I had begun a book which was to contain everything I knew and thought I knew, and on which, as I sensed even then, I would have to spend most of my life), as much as I dreaded the irregularities, circumstances, and changes that a stranger necessarily brings to a house, and especially someone like Tullipan would surely bring, yet I loved him even more and felt that I could not get along without him. Soon Tullipan had become used to me and in short order turned the house upside down. He poked through every nook and cranny; while I was trying as usual to work before noon, I could hear Tullipan moving about up in the attic or down in the cellar, through the rooms of the house, or around on the outside. I was aware of heavy steps, growling, whistling or singing, loud outbursts of laughter here and there, or I heard sudden, quick stomping on the stairs, the creaking of closet doors, trunk lids, drawers, and shutters, the sliding of heavy objects across the tiles; all of the signals of an intense searching and rooting out, noisily, gaily and eerily filled the echoing house. From time to time Tullipan appeared at my desk and struck a pose. Usually he wore a newly-found cap, or showed me shoes, or well-thumbed and long forgotten picture books from my childhood, which I, and I do not know why, had taken from my shelves and packed away somewhere; he brought forth little chests, tools, coasters, cloth and clothing, manuscripts, books and picture frames, empty inkwells, and any number of things which seemed precious to him and which he wanted to keep. I needed only to nod or shake my head and Tullipan

took the objects aside and stowed them away in his chests and
cartons, or, trembling with disappointment, put them back
where he had found them.

A pair of white gloves he had found in a forgotten case and
immediately put on was a constant source of pleasure to him.
He held them up to me, and at the nod of my head wore them
from then on as one of his prize possessions. For the next few
days he could not be coaxed to take them off. Even at meals,
especially at meals, he wore those gloves, which by then had
become covered with filth. Together we had fixed up a large
room on the top floor of the house (most of the rooms stood
empty or were sparsely filled with crates, travelling gear, and
stacks of books), a room where he had been in the habit of
going and which he liked best of all the rooms in the house. In
it we had arranged a wide bed, an old wash stand, and some
book shelves, and had hung a few old-fashioned engravings
(some he had found in the house, others he had rummaged
for at the shop), before which he spent much time, his face
pressed close to the mildewed paper, carefully studying every
detail. It seemed to astound and delight him to find again and
again in the same places those copied objects, the clouds and
coastal cliffs, sailing ships, whales and lighthouses, the
interior scenes and tiny women and groups of people with
their coaches and walking-sticks and the dark silhouettes of
unknown families and their patriarchs. And although he
clearly did not understand the contents of the pictures, he
never asked me about their meaning, and I do not know what
he might have read into them and rediscovered each time.

He took all of the found, stolen, begged, and collected
things to his room and stacked and heaped them according to
his own system of order. In a short time his room was
transformed into a fabulous junkshop and armoury of
remarkable toys. Knick-knacks and fragile objects he tended
with love above all others, packing them into shoe boxes,
soap cartons, orange crates and burlap bags. He collected
tiny pictures from oatmeal and chocolate boxes; postcards
and envelopes, brightly adorned with their stamps, post
marks and addresses; and wine corks, medicine bottles,
pocket calendars, and crumbled cigars, he carried them all
around in the pockets of his bathrobe. And once he brought
home a gramophone (that time I neglected to ask where it

came from) and we got hold of some records — tangos, waltzes, hit tunes, and old overtures — which he played all day long crouching before the machine, and to which he loved to dance. Whenever Tullipan danced, the entire house quaked and rumbled. Often I stood in the doorway of his room and watched; gracefully he wheeled his heavy body between the chests and piles, across the open stretches of floor, balled his fists and stamped in march time, shadow-boxed about or spun so hard and fast that he flew dizzily against a wall. While dancing and stomping he bared his teeth, panted heavily, rolled his eyes and came at me, conjuring from a crouch. Sometimes both of us danced through the house, to stop only when boxes toppled, laughing and exhausted on the stairway, throwing ourselves into nearby chairs until thoughts of food and visions of smoked ham, cigarettes, and coffee drove us to our feet once more.

Even with the ever-increasing numbers of large and small objects his room did not become more disordered. Things that were of equal importance (and they could be of the most diverse value and nature) he heaped onto the same piles; he had perhaps ten of them in his room, and treated each one differently. He shoved his most prized possessions under his bed and rarely took them out. He bothered with sorting and ordering, dividing and ranking, only when no space was left for him on the floor. Nothing Tullipan did revealed far-reaching plans and designs, and none of his actions were predictable. He did not wash regularly in the morning or evening, but only when he felt dirty. And when he did wash, he staged a veritable flood, turning on every faucet, pouring buckets of water over his head, snorting, ranting, sputtering, laughing and sloshing water everywhere, standing breathless and dripping in swiftly spreading puddles, then running naked through the house until he was dry.

Tullipan had claimed many of the things I needed every day, and he turned them over reluctantly with an unhappy face when I missed them and asked him, demanding that he fetch them. In the end I simply let him have whatever he had claimed, even if what I needed was mine, and I just borrowed back what I had to have as the occasion arose. This arrangement seemed to please him, and he was quick to bring what I asked for and then to take it back.

Tullipan loved his room, and what made it especially precious to him was the window. It was possible to look out across the neighbouring roofs right down to the sea, take in an expanse of the broad beach stretching straight to the south, with the great open sky above. Tullipan stood at the window for hours, talking to himself, immersed in the view of the heavens and sea. Whenever he caught sight of the tankers, yachts, barges, or one of the white police-boats that passed by regularly, he hurriedly called me to the window. He pointed out his discoveries with his fingers, explaining that tankers carry houses, horses, and trees, cats and fish from here to there. And the huge, deep-voiced steamers, passing brilliant and shimmering in the sun or on rainy days indistinct like scaly chimeras, were in reality not boats at all. Tullipan never said what they actually were. But they were not steamers or ships. In their smoke stacks and on their bridges sat thick-bodied old men smoking pipes as big as barrels, writing on the tiniest of typewriters the labels for the marmalade jars in the store. And people, visible on the beach for short lengths of time, local residents or tourists racing to and fro at the edge of the sea with dogs and children, small, dark, singly or in groups, struggling against the wind, they were apparitions and beings, probably related to the figures in the engravings, who actually lived in the sea, citizens of foreign royal courts and undersea domains. 'You know, there really are people,' said Tullipan, 'who don't live here, don't wear hats, who have gold things on their heads that make you do this . . .' (Tullipan put his hands over his eyes) '. . . so you don't get a pain in your eyes.' According to him they were ashore only by chance and visible only now and then to us up here.

But the most remarkable thing to Tullipan was the sea he looked at through his window. For him that sea behind the window was not the same as the one he ran into and from which he was able to snatch stones and fish. The sea in his window filled him with wonder and fear. The sea in the windows, the hushed, mostly grey, unreachable sea, was more closely related to the pictures on his wall than to the body of rolling water five hundred yards away. The sea that he could actually experience, that soaked and cooled him,

refreshed and broke over him in booming waves became one
with him on contact and he forgot it. But it was impossible to
touch the sea in the window; mysteriously, stubbornly, it
kept a distance that could not be overcome or forgotten . . .
It could not be used, just looked at calmly from behind the
glass. The sea in Tullipan's pictures never changed, the
objects in the fore-, the middle-, or the background always
remained the same. The sea and the objects Tullipan looked
at through his window also stayed at a distance, and he could
not move among them (so, too, with the pictures), but they
did frequently change (unlike the pictures) and there were
things in the fore-, middle-, and background that shifted,
moved off, suddenly appeared or disappeared. It was a
mystery, working a magic which Tullipan, inextricably
bound within its spell, simply accepted. On many days the
sea in the window was present only in the sound of its waves.
Tullipan spoke with it, addressed himself to it, waved at it,
giving it vague names, and that the sea moved and yet gave no
answer and in no way revealed whether it had heard him, was
and remained the incomprehensible feature that he loved and
feared. The sea in the window was Tullipan's greatest
wonder.

A day full of sun and wind by the sea.
    It is midday and the water is showing its brightest colours,
a clear, sparkling, translucent green with undulating flecks of
rich gold. It overcomes him, Tullipan, the sea. The distant,
roaring sound, the muffled thunder, the sharp smell of kelp
and rotting fish, of cork and grass drives him mad, the
strong, crisp wind has touched him. Tullipan bellows,
throws his arms in the air, and bolts from my side into the
sea, pitches and falls, striking headlong into the brown water
foaming with sand, he rolls through it in his clothes, the tall
hat flips from his head and dips away back and forth on the
waves; Tullipan is laughing, I am left standing on the beach,
completely forgotten, he laughs and screams, gulps water
and spews it out in long streams, he beats at the foam with his
fists, tries to get to his feet, falls over again and thrashes
around on all fours, his knees digging at the shifting sand, he
reels out into the water and crouches, it comes up to his chest,
he gropes at the sandy bottom and snatches up water and bits

of fine gravel, lets it all run from his outstretched hands and
claps it onto his head. He plunges his head into the foam,
stirring and shaking it around; and at last, laughing and
coughing, he collapses, crawls into shallower water, stretches
out, and heaps sand on his belly and legs. Suddenly he
remembers me, waves half-erect and laughs at me, chokes
and coughs hard, his back arched. He rises up, shakes
himself, staggers out of the water, dripping and caked with
white and brown sand, collapses next to me, looks up,
beaming, wipes the water from his face and flings it from his
hand, then sees his hat tossing in the sea not far away, and
throws himself into the waves again to bring it back.

I often pondered how old Tullipan could be. I did not know
and do not know even now, I estimated him to be about
twenty, perhaps a little older. But why should I ask about his
age. Tullipan had no age. Tullipan was Tullipan, and there is
nothing more to be said.

He moves through my house, the neighbourhood, the entire
area just as he pleases, and whatever he does, he does openly,
hiding nothing. Time is strange to him, he cannot grasp it. In
the middle of the night he often goes singing out of the house,
or he jumps up suddenly during a meal because something
has popped into his head and struck his fancy, and dashes
off, and I finish eating alone. Darkness gives him no reason to
sleep or even to rest. He goes to sleep when he is tired,
wherever he is.
    I am awakened by him one night. He is tickling my ears.
    'You know,' he says, 'the shop is not friendly. I was down
there a while ago and there is no one around and everything's
locked up. And nobody comes, although I'm standing there
and waiting, and knock and call for somebody to open up,
because I'd like to go in and get something. Cookies, you
know, and all that, and sausage. But no one comes to open
up. Then somebody pops out next door and says I've got to
go home, back to your place I should go, or wherever I
belong, the shop won't open up, he says. And it didn't,
either.'
    'Yes,' I say, 'the store is not open at night. It's closed.
People are asleep and do not sell things because everyone else

C Michel € 1964   halber Engel   2/2

is asleep too and no one wants anything. They do their buying and selling during the day. That is all arranged. There are little signs saying it is so. And people abide by those little signs. See, even I sleep at night and shop during the day. Everyone around here is asleep, except those people who are at sea catching fish.'

'But I did see someone,' says Tullipan, 'he wasn't asleep. There was a light on in this place, I went right in where it was. It caught my eye right away, it was the only light I saw.'

'Did you meet anyone?' I ask.

'Yes, I met somebody inside,' he says, 'but he wasn't about to talk very long, he had something to do. So I just watched.'

'That must have been the shoemaker,' I say, 'he always works at night, everyone knows that.'

'Yes, he was making shoes,' says Tullipan, 'sitting around amongst all those shoes, pounding on one of them. Beautiful shoes, but too small for me.'

'Did you try on any of them,' I ask.

'No, I didn't,' says Tullipan, 'I saw right off they were too small.' Tullipan laughs. 'Much too small. So small!' And he shows me with his fingers how small the shoes were.

'Well, Tullipan,' I say, 'you can go shopping tomorrow. Let's get some sleep now, we are both tired.'

'Ahhh,' says Tullipan with a long sigh, 'I want to sleep right now, I really do, I'm tired too, yes. Even the stone is asleep, did you see?'

'The stone, it might be asleep,' I say, 'I don't know if it is. Perhaps it is asleep, perhaps it isn't, perhaps it sleeps only during the day.'

Tullipan dashes off and, from its resting place next to the sofa in my study, fetches the stone that he gave me as a gift when he first arrived, and holds it up before my face.

'Asleep,' asks Tullipan, 'or isn't he?'

I touch the stone. 'He's asleep,' I answer.

'You see, he is sleeping,' says Tullipan and on tip-toes carries it from the room.

The next day I go about and put everything in order as best I can. (I had given Tullipan some money and explained how to use it, but he had put it away in one of his boxes and not spent a cent.) I walk to the store and tell the old woman that she is to give Tullipan whatever he comes for and is to charge it to me.

'That'll be pretty expensive for you,' says the old woman.

'It does not matter,' I answer, 'everything will work out.'

'As you wish,' she mutters, 'your visitor comes in almost every day and takes a pound or so of this and that, I'm only saying it will cost you a pretty penny . . .'

'And,' I say, 'he can get anything he wants, I'll pay for it.'

'Of course, just as you wish,' she says. 'Agreed. But it won't do to have him coming around at night, rousting everybody out of bed.'

'Just this once,' I say, 'you could overlook that. He doesn't know how things are done around here, but he will soon get used to them.'

And I walk over to the shoemaker's shop and apologize, but he says it does not bother him if somebody stops in at night, actually he enjoys it. He listens to the radio when he's working at night anyway.

'Good,' I say, 'and if he does disturb you, just tell him to leave. If you speak in a friendly way, he will leave at once, he understands that much; he's a good fellow and will understand.'

And so on. And I go to the people from whom he took the sandals and explain that he meant no harm, he can be trusted, that otherwise he is a fine lad, and he could return the sandals.

They are not that important, I am told, they were hardly missed, and no one thought that my visitor . . . and he was the one who . . . ?

And so on. I leave word at the tavern that I will stand good for all of Tullipan's bills. 'From what I hear,' I say, 'Tullipan comes in now and then?'

'Yes, he drops in here often,' says the manager. 'Drops in, that's good! Him dropping in! Does it up right, he does, just pours it down. Any idea how much your visitor can take?' And he produces a few bar tabs he has saved for me. I pay them.

'Out of his head when he's drunk,' says a beer drinker at the bar.

'He's out of his head when he's sober, heh-heh,' says someone from a corner table.

Loud laughter. 'Guzzles whatever is dumped into his glass,' says the beer drinker.

'Ha, I'd say he's batty, that one,' says someone else.

'You've got something there,' says the manager.

Tullipan continues to carry things into his room. At last it turns out to be too small, and he starts new piles in an adjoining room. The days have grown warm, the doors and windows stand open, Tullipan has been with me now for several weeks. Each day he gives me some kind of present, a feather, an old newspaper, cigarettes, coffee beans, chocolate eggs (he has found out that they can be eaten), pennies, and stones. Each morning he dashes to the post office and brings me letters and papers, he goes to the store for my cigarettes, and, whenever he is around, takes care of the shopping without a word from me. Day after day he asks what I am reading in the newspaper (Tullipan can neither read nor write) and listens absently with an open mouth as I tell that turmoil and war are raging here and there, coming ever closer, and could crush even our house. I explain what wars and uprisings are and show him photographs of people involved in war, unrest, hunger, death, and hatred, and I show him photos of those who are trying to work against such things. Tullipan takes the paper, studies the photographs, investigating wars and the people involved, and comprehends nothing. He asks me if the sea will leave if there is war, and when I say no, he is satisfied.

Every day he puts new things on the table for me to appreciate and admire. It is extraordinarily important to him that I praise his valuables and discoveries lavishly. If I do find fault with something about them and say, perhaps, 'What is that good for,' or 'Whatever are you going to do with this dirty little thing here,' he hesitates, holding the objects uncertainly, quietly in his hands, then laughs and looks pleadingly at me for indulgence, the joy he takes in his belongings causes him to forget my objection, and he carries them carefully away.

During these weeks I have not made progress with my work. My book lies in my desk drawer, a heap of scribbled pages. I try to do something every day and struggle with a tighter

schedule to help myself along, but that does not work. I lack
peace and concentration. Tullipan is always nearby, laughing
and generous with his bubbling joy and cheerfulness, he
continually discovers new reasons to talk to me, to divert and
delight me. And since he cannot be made to understand that I
am working, that it is something I want and have to do and
simply cannot be interrupted so casually while I am at it, I
often lose patience and speak crossly to Tullipan. When this
happens, he retreats, hurt, to his room with sorrow on his
face. But we make up again while we are eating and drinking,
playing music, or singing. And I walk to the post office and
telephone for an extension of my deadline.

One evening Tullipan comes home, hangs around out in the
hall, and stops, finally, in the doorway of my room, making a
gloomy face.

'Come in, Tullipan,' I say, 'get something to eat from the
kitchen.'

'I don't want to,' says Tullipan.

'But you are so sullen,' I say, 'what has become of your
laugh? Tell me, if there is anything to tell.'

'I got into a scuffle,' says Tullipan.

'Oh,' I say, 'tell me your troubles.'

'Oh, I didn't start it,' he yells excitedly, 'I was just sitting
in the little house.'

'Whose privy were you using,' I ask.

'The one belonging to the store in Meerstrasse. I ran right
in, fast, because I was right there and in a hurry, and because
I didn't know any other place. I've been there many times
before. And I sat in there a little while, and then the woman
from the shop came in . . .'

'Didn't you lock the door?' I ask.

'I guess I forgot,' says Tullipan and thinks back. 'All at
once the door flew open and there she was, coming in, but she
didn't . . .'

'You must have been singing,' I say. 'The woman from the
shop is not used to hearing songs in her privy, most likely it is
always quiet, and she was just coming to see who could be
singing in there.'

'Wasn't singing at all,' says Tullipan reproachfully, 'just
sitting quietly in the little house, you know, thinking

nothing. She just came right in. But all turned around,'
shouts Tullipan, 'with her bottom first she was coming in,
Right at me. Well, I just sat there and she's coming closer and
closer, and I couldn't figure out what to do, it was all
happening so fast, and she had her dress up in her hands,
coming at me with her bum. And I know why. She always
goes in that way. She's just too fat, said so herself afterwards,
she said it so mean, she can't turn around in there, she said,
and wasn't friendly at all. So she always has to go in
backwards and plops down when she gets to the seat. But I
was sitting there myself and thinking, now, if she's going to
come in and sit, she'll squeeze me right down into the hole.
And when she was almost on top of me, I hauled off and hit
her. A couple of quick ones, right there, and she took off with
a howl, and so fast! She was in such a scramble to get away,
she crashed into the wall and little white spots rubbed off all
over her clothes, and her skirt fell down again.'

Tullipan looks at me gravely, upset. 'Then what did you
do?' I ask.

'I finished up,' says Tullipan, 'went out. There she was,
standing in the yard, looking at me cock-eyed and squinty,
snorting and telling me off loud and fast, and louder than all
else she yelled: pig! And said I should go away as fast as I can,
too. And she said all that with such a threat, that I did, I got
right out. And I came running straight here.'

'What do I do now,' asks Tullipan. 'I can't go back there
any more, from now on you'll have to get our things.' He
looks at me woefully.

'Ummm, what will we do now,' I say.

'Nothing, we'll do nothing,' I say. 'Nothing at all. We shall
forget your troubles and not do a thing.'

'Do you know what I found today,' calls Tullipan. Breathing
heavily he lopes noisily into the room, plants himself in front
of me, and looks on expectantly. Glistening streams of sweat
roll down his temples into his collar, he is tired and happy, his
hat is crumpled, the belt of his bathrobe drags the floor and
his tennis shoes are marked with dark rings of dried and dirty
water.

'Well, what have you found,' I say, 'show me, Tullipan!'

'It's on its way now,' he says, 'come over and stand by the

window, then you'll see it as soon as it comes.' Both of us stand at the open window and wait.

'Where have you been, Tullipan?' I ask.

'Back there, you know, in the mountains,' he says.

'The first time you've been there,' I say, 'then you found your way without any trouble?'

'There's nothing to it,' says Tullipan. 'I just went right into the mountains and then up on them. It wasn't hard to find, you can see them everywhere. You can't go astray. You can always look at the sea and find it. And the same with the mountains.'

'Did you see the large river?' I ask.

'Yes, I saw it,' says Tullipan, 'so beautiful. I even went into it, had to get through. It is dark blue back in there, but goes faster and faster off to one side. Carries its water right down into the sea. Where it comes out, I don't know yet, I'll have to look sometime.'

As we stand at the window waiting and talking about the river and the mountains, evening slowly falls. A cool, brown twilight slips across the yard, over the grass, pushing the great mountains far back into the sky.

'Just guess what I've found,' says Tullipan.

'A goat,' I say.

'A goat,' roars Tullipan with delight. 'Hohoho, nonono! Haa!' He beats his fists on the windowsill with joy, and laughs. 'Hshshsh, shsh, shsh. A goat! Not a goat!'

'Then perhaps a . . . tree stump,' I say, 'or a rooster, or a bird's egg or perhaps a signal from along the railroad tracks?'

'Oh no, no,' shouts Tullipan, laughing and laughing, 'no rooster and nothing from the railroad. Something else. Something much different. You won't guess it, ever.'

'Then I'll just have to wait a while,' I say, 'until you show me.' And Tullipan, pleased that I have not been able to guess, stands next to me and we wait in the growing darkness for whatever is supposed to appear.

After half an hour finally we hear something coming. We hear footsteps and the grating of wheels behind the house. Indistinct in the darkness two men in broad-brimmed hats appear in the front yard of the house, pulling into the circle of light from the windows a cart on which, resting lengthwise on the narrow bed, lies a dark, coffin-like wooden mass. We fetch flashlights and go out front to look at the object — an enormous, three-legged, dark-grained, intricately carved upright clock.

Tullipan looks into my face, proud but embarrassed.

'I found it,' he says. 'And these are my friends.' In turn both men, dumpy labourers in dungarees and work jackets, shake my hand. I ask if they would like something to eat and drink.

The men mutter something, but not in an unfriendly way, and follow me into the house. 'Yes,' says Tullipan, 'and for me and you, too, something to eat and drink. Give them something to eat, much to eat! I'll get it.' And Tullipan dashes off, and I think to myself, he is going to the kitchen and getting us something to eat and drink.

'Sit down, won't you,' I say, and pull up chairs and make a place on the table for what bottles there are in the room. 'The best is yet to come!'

The two men remove their hats and wipe the sweat from their faces with large, checkered handkerchiefs. They sit down rather stiffly and pull out tobacco tins and cigarette papers.

'A very nice piece of work,' says the heavier of the two, and his companion nods thoughtfully.

'Where did he get it, the clock,' I ask, 'do you know?'

'Where he got it?' The heavier man shrugs his shoulders and looks at me. 'He was half carrying, half dragging it and something else. A funny sight. I think he was coming down from the mountains. And he asked if he could get a cart from us for his two things, and we had a cart, but to us he looked a bit, well, a touch off his track, you know, and we figured we'd better stay with the cart. It belongs to the sawmill on the other side of the river. We thought we'd come along and pick up a little extra cash. We had plenty of time, and he ran on ahead, told us just to follow the road, and he stopped and showed us where to go.'

'How did you get the cart across the river?' I ask.

'On the railroad bridge,' says the smaller man, nodding.

'Lucky, too,' says the other, 'there was no train coming right then, we would've had to make haste like fleas on a dog with those rails. Something did happen, though.'

I ask what happened.

'One of the things, those clock things, slid off the wagon, we just couldn't hold it and it fell right off the bridge. Your friend didn't want to keep going, but we told him we'd leave him standing if he didn't come along, and so he kept going. I think he's already forgotten about it. He let out such a screech when that thing dropped into the river.'

As I am paying the two men, Tullipan returns, his arms full of ham slices, bread, and bottles. Exhaling, he puts everything on to the table, and we begin eating and drinking.

After a while, Tullipan, chewing: 'Where do you think we can put the clock? It's too big for the parlour.'

'We shall have to think about that,' I say.

'Maybe right there on the hearth,' Tullipan says. 'I can see it all the time, there's nothing to get in the way and you can see it fine.'

'But then the smoke would not go up the chimney,' I say, 'and we would be left sitting in smoke, coughing all the time.'

'Well, then,' says Tullipan, 'it would be best by the sea where there's plenty of room.' He is thinking. 'But I don't get down there very often. I can't always be running down there. Just to look at the clock, because it's not right here.'

'The best place for it is out in front of the house,' I suggest, 'and we shall put up a roof to keep off the rain.' That suits Tullipan, and after we have finished eating, we move out to the yard — the two men stay at the table and continue eating — lift the clock down from the cart, stand it up little by little, work stones and clods of earth beneath its base, test its steadiness, nail a piece of tarpaper on top, and even discover a key inside the housing with which we wind the clock. It begins ticking at once, a deep-throated gong sounds nine times. The men have come to the window and laugh at us when they see us working with the clock.

Tullipan begins to race and dance around it, I return to the men in the house, leaving him alone in the darkness with his new friendship.

Oppressive heat had descended upon land and sea. In the morning the mountains sank back into dense blue colours and only their upper outlines were visible between earth and sky in the distance. Middays were stifling, and their light was smoky white. Nights cooled but little. The wind came now from the land, now from the sea, constant, hot and steady, and the heat did not change for many weeks. During the day the doors and windows of the house were shut while the wind raced across the front yard, swirled dust, and powdered fine sand through the air. The windows and doors stood open at night. I worked little during this time. Tullipan roamed the area for days and nights on end, mostly by the sea and in the mountains, I rode my bicycle in the early morning hours through the bottom land, and once we set off with a knapsack full of supplies and were two days on the road. I considered taking a longer trip, but thoughts of Tullipan held me back.

Tullipan had traded his tall black hat for a honey-coloured sun visor that sat above his eyes like a crescent moon; and he now was dashing about in an old white vest and wore wooden clogs in place of his tennis shoes, and their clatter usually awoke me in the morning. Dark cloud formations often showed above the sea. Thunderstorms passed in the distance. And the days were full.

One night during a violent thunderstorm I wake up and hear Tullipan's voice in the hall and a voice I do not know. I get up and go out. Tullipan, squinting with fatigue, is sitting on the steps with a stranger. He had a broad, red face in which his eyes, small and black, are sticking like tacks. A stocking cap on his head. Pale red shirt, faded and tattered in places. Work pants. Sandals.

'Oh, there you are,' says Tullipan, as I step from my room. 'Look, here he is,' Tullipan says to the stranger. With difficulty the man stands up, groaning a little, and extends his hand. He mumbles something I cannot make out.

'We were just wondering if we'd better wake you up, or just keep the noise down because you were sleeping.'

'I just now woke up,' I say, 'it was a clap of thunder, not you; you are both soaked, you need something to drink.'

'Down by the bridge the rain really cut loose,' says the stranger, 'and your friend said it wasn't far to his place. We ran all the way.'

'Fridolin is his name,' says Tullipan. 'He's my friend!' And he glances back and forth, from my face to his.

Rain rattles and slaps on the porch steps that are cast in gold by the hall light shining through the half-open door.

Wind blows from all angles through the house, bluish flashes crease the sky above the sea, for split seconds outside in the yard broad puddles can be seen, splashing and churning in the driving rain, and grass in lashing clumps and the dark outline of the clock.

'Come in,' I say, 'and change into something dry.' I fetch jackets and towels, Tullipan and Fridolin dry themselves, yawning and groaning, then cognac and bread are brought to the table, and bacon, eggs, and coffee.

'We took a little tour of the taverns, you know,' says Fridolin, and Tullipan nods gravely, sluggishly, from the sofa.

'You can't tell at all,' I say.

A fit of soundless laughter appears on Fridolin's red face, and Tullipan, shaking with giggles, squirms on the sofa. 'Heh, heh, heh . . . you can't tell anything,' he sings, 'can't tell anything! *You* can't tell anything,' he mumbles between two bursts of laughter. '*You!* but everybody else could, wherever we went . . .' And laughs and laughs.

'I've got to agree there,' chuckles Fridolin, 'but I think the rain's washed some of it away.'

Tullipan's laughter ends in a short volley of coughs. He grows silent and absently eyes first one, then the other. We eat and drink and strain our ears at the pummelling rain.

'You have many books,' says Fridolin after a while, looking about the room, 'I have ten at most.'

'I've picked them up in the course of time,' I say, 'and now, altogether, there is quite a collection.'

'I see you even have one by Jennessy,' says Fridolin.

'I read it often,' I answer, 'I have a few of his books, that's true, mostly his poems. Do you know Jennessy's work?'

'Yes, I do,' says Fridolin, 'some of his poems.'

I look more closely at Fridolin. He could be about fifty years old. He is stuffing huge pieces of ham into his mouth. I am amazed, he knows poems by Jennessy.

'Otherwise, I don't know any other poet,' says Fridolin, 'but I have read him. Even know a few of his things by heart, if I haven't forgotten them by now.'

'How did you get started on his poetry?' I ask. Tullipan eyes his coffee sleepily.

'I found them once, some poems,' says Fridolin, 'a book

by Jennessy was lying around somewhere, and I started reading because there was nothing else, left part behind, took part along. Whatever became of it, by God, I just don't know any more. I usually don't read poems, but these were really good.'

'Few people are familiar with Jennessy's poems,' I say, 'that's why I was surprised that you had read any of them.'

Fridolin shrugs his shoulders indifferently, Tullipan, who has been listening, so it seems, lowers his head again and licks at his coffee mug.

'He is not very popular,' I say, 'but a few people are beginning to read what he writes.'

'So, he's still alive,' says Fridolin, 'I always thought he had to be an old dead poet from long ago.'

'No, Jennessy is alive,' I answer, 'he lives two hundred miles north of here. He is not very old, perhaps fifty.'

'My, my, so he is still alive,' mumbles Fridolin, nodding with surprise and a heavy head. 'You really cannot tell when you read him, you would think he lived much earlier.'

Tullipan has been listening with glazed and wandering eyes. 'Do you know him personally?' asks Fridolin. I shake my head.

Fridolin nods sluggishly and concentrates again on cutting his ham. I attempt to bring Fridolin to say more about Jennessy, but he has just finished eating, is getting drowsy, and yawns. We lift Tullipan, who has fallen asleep, from the sofa and carry him into his room. The rain is still falling fast and thick. Fridolin spends the night on the sofa. The next morning Tullipan and Fridolin have disappeared.

Tullipan was increasingly on the move. And he was drunk more often. He continued collecting things and carrying them to his room, but his heart, it seemed to me, was not in it. I pondered whether I actually knew what Tullipan did and where he spent his time. I was working from five to seven hours each day, and for the first time since Tullipan's appearance, I felt confident that I was making progress in my work.

I am coming back from the city one night on my bicycle, after visiting friends, delivering manuscripts, and buying paper, it is near morning, and I am riding slowly toward home. In the weak beam of my light I see someone lying face down in the middle of Meerstrasse. I get down from my bike and turn him over on his back: It is Tullipan. He is snoring, half asleep, talking under his breath. A sharp stench of cheap liquor hangs over him.

'Tullipan,' I say, gently slapping his cold cheeks, 'what is the matter with you, come on, move around a little, don't be so silly. Try to stand up.'

Jarred from his sleep, Tullipan shakes his head, struggling up on his elbows, lifts his head, and looks at me slack-jawed out of swollen eyes.

'No,' he screams when he recognizes me, and shoves me weakly away with his fists as he falls back, he flops over on to his belly and lowers his head to the pavement. 'No! No!'

'Come on, stand up, Tullipan,' I say softly, 'it is not good to lie around in the streets at night, come along. Come on now, stand up . . .'

'I don't want to,' he bellows. 'No!'

'I'm on my way home, I say, 'wouldn't you rather come with me?'

'No! All of you, oh . . . !' He looks coldly and sadly into my eyes. 'You know, I don't want to,' he says quietly, hanging his head.

'I don't want to, no, I don't want to,' he bellows suddenly, 'I . . . don't . . . want . . . to . . . !' He rolls over a few times and stops with a thud against the wall of a house. I stand uncertainly in the street, holding my bicycle. From the jerking of his shoulders I realize finally that he is crying. 'Go . . . go away,' he says, his voice barely audible between sobs.

I stand there a while, not knowing what to do. Never before have I seen Tullipan cry. And I push my bike toward home.

Since that night Tullipan has changed greatly. Yet even earlier I had often noticed a kind of uncertainty, a sullen stubbornness, but I had given it little thought.

Now he was away from home most of the time and no longer told me what he had done and where he had been. He had become restless and pensive and spoke only when necessary. Whenever he did come home, he seemed beaten down and distant; he still brought me the mail every day, but he did not lay it on my table with a laugh, as if giving me a marvellous, valuable gift, instead, he pushed it quietly up onto the ledge from outside the window or slipped it into my room under the door. I thanked him loudly whenever I heard him running through the hall and called out his name, but he stayed out of sight and slipped away again. Tullipan had become reticent in everything he did.

I did not even know where to start with him, I was troubled and ill-at-ease. The shoemaker said that Tullipan hadn't been to see him in some time. And only once in a while did he go to the store and he was seldom seen on Meerstrasse.

'He just stands by the sea for hours on end and stares at the water, your visitor,' said the old woman in the store.

'Yes, I know,' I said.

He avoided the tavern completely. And, I discovered, they had thrown him out the same night I found him sprawled drunk on Meerstrasse. He had insisted on staying and drinking, and there had been a fight between him and the manager and a few late drinkers.

'Naturally, that won't do,' said the manager, 'I can't stay open all night on his account. I lock up by one o'clock at the latest. He can have as much as he wants, but he'll have to drink it somewhere else.'

'You could do nothing about it, of course not,' I said.

'God knows, you really don't know what to do with a fellow like that,' said the manager.

What in addition and in particular happened to Tullipan I could not discover. There was only vague talk about him, and, it seemed to me, people were keeping their thoughts and opinions to themselves. Because of Tullipan, there had been frequent fights in the neighbourhood, he had been baited and ridiculed just to see how he would respond. Everything I was able to learn fed my growing suspicion that Tullipan was not well liked and that many people had been out to get him.

The fact that he was so vulnerable, that he could not continue to live the way he did, and that there were people who always found fault with him, laughed at him, and called him an idiot, the fact that he could be hurt deeply, and had been hurt deeply, may have been the single thing that Tullipan had come to understand since he came to live with me. He raced and ran about and then disappeared some-where near the sea or in the stunted woods along the river. Sorrow and rebellion were in his eyes. He avoided me and everyone else, and I did not know how I could have helped him.

'What is the matter, Tullipan?' I ask, coming home one day at noon to find him sitting, dozing in the open doorway. 'Come in,' I say, 'we shall cook something you like, we'll drink something special.' Tullipan follows me to the kitchen and we fry fish and, standing up in the kitchen, we eat bread and fish.

'I'm going to leave,' says Tullipan, not looking up from his plate, and he shifts his weight nervously from one foot to the other.

'And you do want to go away,' I say, 'why do you want to leave, just tell me, Tullipan. This comes as a great surprise.'

'No surprise at all,' he says, and stares at his plate, picking at his fish with his fork. 'I've wanted to leave for some time.'

'Where do you want to go,' I ask, lifting two more fish on to my plate. 'Now look, it is late in the summer, the weather will not be warm much longer. The sea is already turning cold, the wind is colder, too, and soon the rains will come. It is not a good time to leave, Tullipan.'

'That doesn't matter,' he says, 'whether it's warm or cold, I'm going, tomorrow I am leaving.'

'And do you know why?' he asks, leaning forward, looking me gloomily in the face, and he puts his plate on the stove.

'Oh, I'd rather not say, you know,' he says, then glances down at his shoes, and reaches for his plate. We eat our fish in silence.

'I can tell you why,' I answer then, 'I think I know. Because you have been laughed at here, treated brutally and badly, because a few people shout after you: Holy Smoke, look at that freak! Well, for heaven's sake, what a character, what a screwball! Isn't that right, Tullipan? And because there are a few people who say right to your face: you stink of booze, my boy, you wear silly hats and idiotic shoes. Isn't that right?'

Tullipan raised his head and looks at me without any expression on his face.

'And someone comes along and asks why you've got those gloves on, and in summer, too, and the shoemaker says you are not to touch the shoes, they are women's shoes, he says, and don't fool with them, he says your fingers are too greasy. And in the tavern somebody starts sniping at you the moment you walk through the door, and they come up to you at the bar and ask such ludicrous, senseless things and then laugh behind your back, vilely at times. And the bartender says you have to go home, he wants to close up, and you shouldn't drink so much, or at least do it somewhere else. And all in all people are not as friendly to you as you are to them, not as friendly as you would like them to be. Isn't that right, Tullipan?'

Tullipan chews his fish and nods a few times.

'Listen to me, Tullipan,' I say, 'that is all out of proportion, unimportant, petty, do not worry your head about it, it is utter nonsense,' I say, cautiously touching his arm, 'look, in any case you do know . . .'

Tullipan shakes his head. 'There's something else,' he says.

I am out of breath from talking so much and look at him questioningly.

'You,' he says and lowers his head. 'You, too! You won't treat me right, either, not you or any of the others. You always have to work, always, always. You don't go with me any more, even to the mountains. Oh yes, once you came along, yes, once. And you only go with me to the sea because it's so near. But no farther. And you tell me I have to give back this or that, you need it, and not to run around in my wooden shoes and make noise,' he looks at me coldly, and his voice grows louder, 'and the window, keep it closed, there's a draught, and don't sing outside at night, or kick stones in the street, don't do that either, and everything I've found,' he thumps his chest and jerks his head accusingly, 'I have found, I'm supposed to take right back and can't keep it even a little while . . .'

'Tullipan,' I say, 'please listen to me, listen to me for a minute, please . . .'

'No,' bellows Tullipan, 'no! no! I can't do anything around here. I don't want to stay, no. I'm leaving, I'm leaving right now!'

He slams down his plate and a few pieces of fish, some bones, and bread tumble across the floor.

'You can have it all,' he yells, 'everything, everything!' He throws his arms wildly about. 'And I'm giving you everything, keep it, yes, just keep it. I don't want any part of it, no, I don't even want to be here . . .'

'Tullipan,' I say calmly, 'you shouldn't scream like that when we're alone. It's not like that at all, you must believe me.'

'I'm not supposed to scream,' he bellows, 'you always say that, I'm not supposed to! I shouldn't scream, shouldn't do anything! Just keep my mouth shut, always do something else than what I'm doing, that's all I ever hear.'

Then Tullipan grows quiet. 'I'm leaving,' he says tonelessly.

'I'm going, do you hear,' he calls. He strides toward the door. 'I'll shut the door,' he screams, 'so there won't be any draught! There!' And he softly closes the kitchen door, 'and shut *this* one, too,' he shouts from the hallway, 'so the rain won't come in.' I hear his heavy, thudding steps in front of the house. 'Go ahead and work,' he bellows from outside, 'now go ahead and work.' I hear Tullipan moving off with quick steps.

And Tullipan is gone.

I had figured that Tullipan would come back, but he did not. I had sensed his pain, but never considered it to be so deep and consuming that he would just turn and run off with it. And in the beginning I did not know what I ought to have done differently and what I had in fact done wrong. I thought later that I should have explained everything to him more tactfully and thoroughly. From the beginning I ought to have recognized his real self more clearly, this self of my own creation. Now I realized that I had almost always short-changed him in explanations, respect, and consideration. I owed nothing to the people in the area. Yet again and again I had tried to make them understand how Tullipan had to be handled and what sort of fellow he was, how they should respond to him and so forth. And to these people, who deserved it least of all, I had given everything; but to Tullipan I had given nothing. From the beginning I should never have attempted the hopeless task of making peace between Tullipan and the others on their terms. What did I have to lose, here, in some little corner of the world where I lived as a foreigner, a tourist and writer who was treated politely out of habit and about whom people had their own private thoughts? Nothing! Perhaps at one time I did think I had something to lose. No, I did not. After Tullipan was gone, I realized that I had nothing to lose but him.

At the start I should have said to my creation: 'These people, you see, do not know you very well and never will. They do not understand who you are and who I am and do not want to know. To them you are something strange and out of place, you come from far away where they have never been and will never go. You are different. You probably understand the sea better than any of them who were born here, spend their entire lives here, and will die here. You are so different, but be friendly to them. From time to time they are a little wrong-headed, these people, they are likely to be malicious, hard-nosed, and closed-mouthed, and they like to see someone who does not belong have a bit of bad luck, and they tend to scorn what you love. But whatever they are, they deserve that we, you and I, be kind to them. If they act as though they wanted to make you mad, do not believe them. Simply do not believe them and tell them that you do not believe them. They are just bored,' I ought to have said to Tullipan, 'and you, you are never bored. And it will occur to them that here is someone who is never bored and who knows about things which are commonly taken to be ludicrous and silly. — Just give a slight bow and go on. What does it matter to you if people are the way they are and as they always were and always will be! What does it matter to you, you, this Tullipan who is my creation, my giant, and my headman!'

But Tullipan was gone, and my soul-searching came too late. I blamed myself. How pointless that was now. I had underrated him and not even once looked beneath the surface of my creation. I had ignored all of those crucial, everyday problems. Oh, if I had just let my work go, laughed a little more, and been up to more mischief.

And Tullipan remains lost, days and weeks I wait for him and learn nothing. I am asked at the store if my guest has travelled on.

'He is away again,' I say.

'My, my,' says the old woman, nodding her head.

They miss him at the tavern. 'Toward the last he didn't drop in very often,' says the manager. 'I used to see him once in a while, all out of sorts, running down Meerstrasse. He was always in such a rush. Now he's really gone, for long?'

'Yes, he is gone,' I say, 'I assume for a long time, but I do not know.'

'And he wasn't in such a good mood toward the end?' the man asks.

'That is the impression I got,' I answer.

'Where's he off to now? Where does he really live,' asks the manager.

'He never did give me his address,' I reply.

The weeks slip by and I have not stopped waiting. My work goes ahead, easier and better, I have ample time once more and spend entire days at my typewriter. October has come and I have again started lighting the fire. Heavy rains are falling, the unused rooms of the house have grown damp and cold. Only during midday do I even occasionally open my study window, whenever the sun shines down for a few fleeting hours against the front of the house. I have touched none of Tullipan's things. I did move the clock out of the way to the edge of the yard, but have not wound it. I am hoping that Tullipan will come back sometime.

In the morning I pick up my mail, my newspapers and cigarettes, but I do not expect to hear from Tullipan. Sending letters, or any such form of passing on news, is unknown to him. Tullipan's messages would be his appearance in person. The postmistress, it seems, watches me sceptically out of the corner of her eyes. She does not say much, but I sense everyone can see that I am occupied with something most unusual. Perhaps they do know more about me and Tullipan than I think is possible.

One Sunday morning near the end of October there is a knock on my door and Fridolin steps into the house. He is neatly dressed. Black jacket, black slacks, red shirt. Damp, slicked-down hair. His thick, red neck spills over his red collar. He asks politely how I am and says that he has come to tell us goodbye. He asks if Tullipan is home.

'Come in, Fridolin,' I say.

'Well, where is he,' asks Fridolin and laughs. 'Here!' He lifts his coat and gestures toward a bottle of cognac sticking in his pants pocket. 'I brought a little something for us,' he says, 'something nice.'

'Tullipan is not here,' I say, 'he has gone away.'

'When's he coming back?' asks Fridolin. 'He will be mad if he comes back and finds the bottle empty.'

'I don't know if he will ever come back,' I say.

'What's this,' says Fridolin, 'he's gone? That seems funny.' He shakes his head. 'Been away long?'

'For a few weeks,' I say.

'He didn't say anything about it to me,' says Fridolin, 'not a word.'

'Of course, it is just possible he will come back,' I answer.

'Well,' says Fridolin, 'I would not be too sure. If he's gone, then he's gone. And a few weeks have already passed?'

'So,' I say, 'let's have something to drink.' I fetch glasses and a bottle of plum brandy.

'Allow me,' says Fridolin, pushing my bottle aside, 'I'll take care of this.' We sit down and drink from his bottle.

'He once told me something about the poet, the poet Jennessy,' says Fridolin as we begin to drink. 'He knows him then?'

'I don't think so,' I say, 'I would not know how that could be.'

'He told me that Jennessy lives on a high mountain,' Fridolin begins, 'somewhere on a plateau surrounded by trees, farther to the south. There is a deep, dark lake close by, and huge fish live in it. Tullipan told me. Every morning Jennessy catches a fish from the water and rides around a mountain and up the tallest peak in the region where he has his house. So Tullipan says. At noon he cleans the fish and eats it, drinking a pitcher of the cold, dark lake water. He has a ridiculously large number of squat fat cats that grow broader and fatter on the fish scraps he feeds them. They sit about on his books, his sofa, and his typewriter, and Jennessy has to sing songs, his own, to get them down from his books and typewriter when he wants to use them.'

'Tullipan told you all that?' I ask.

'Word for word,' says Fridolin, 'and with added touches. For example, all of the cats have names, and so on.'

'I am amazed,' I say, 'he hardly ever told me such things. Sometimes he talked a little like that while we were standing at the window, looking down at the sea, but very little and not often, and nothing whatever about Jennessy.'

'He claims Jennessy has two noses,' says Fridolin.

'Jennessy,' I reply, 'lives in a nice house in a large city, he is always well dressed, he lives quietly. He earns his living on the best newspapers we have and delivers radio lectures on literature. He must earn a nice sum, but I think it isn't important to him if he makes a lot or a little. I once saw a photograph of him in an anthology. He is even said to own an automobile. And he does have a nose, just one, that is as normal as any nose can be. And what else did Tullipan tell about?'

'You know, he's a crazy fellow, he is,' says Fridolin. 'He spins the wildest yarns when he's sober, and when he's drunk, he usually does not say a word, just sits and listens. He's really a poet, once he gets started. For example, he claims that the heart of the whale is another whale. And inside the whale that is the heart of the whale, lives another whale, a smaller one. And down inside it is another, and finally, after smaller and smaller whales, in the belly of the very smallest one is a copper chest. In it rests an eye. When the eye closes, the whale dives down in the sea. When the eye opens, the whale comes up again and sprays his water around.'

'Why I had no idea Tullipan was capable of such things,' I say.

'He told me many such things,' says Fridolin.

We talk and drink on into the night, and I ask Fridolin where he is going and what he is doing, and he says he has been cutting wood for a long time, but is looking around for other work, he's getting too old for the forests, he says, but anybody can get a job, anybody, if he wants to. He must move around, he says, otherwise he gets restless, and within the next few days he'll be leaving the region.

'But one of these days,' he says, 'I'll come back through, then I'll look in, and the three of us will sit around the table, Tullipan will be back long since. Then there will be some real drinking,' he says, 'and I think that is how it will be.'

A few weeks pass. In late autumn the colouring of the sea is uncanny. After I have worked and taken care of what needs to be done, I hike and travel along the coast through grey, soundless afternoons, or I go to the city to shop or visit. Many evenings I entertain friends. One of my stories has appeared in the literary section of a newspaper. The postmistress claims she has read it and says that is quite a job I have. The days seem to drift down from the sky and I keep thinking of Tullipan.

Once, while handing me some letters, the postmistress says they know where my guest is.

'Well, it's about time,' I say, and do not have the vaguest notion.

'And they claim he's taken up with a woman,' she says.

'I know nothing of that,' I reply.

'He would have let you know if things had gone that far,' says the postmistress and laughs, pleased; I laugh, too, but rather uncertainly, and really am at a loss. Surely, I think, I would be the first to know Tullipan's whereabouts.

'Why, who is spreading such rumours?' I ask, taking care to be amused.

'The skinny old man, you know,' says the postmistress, 'the one who was in that tractor accident last fall, the one with the crew cut, he knows, he's been talking about it.'

And once I see the skinny man. 'Ho,' I call across the street, 'I have heard you recently saw Tullipan, is that right?' (He knows, of course, my guest from a few weeks ago.)

'Oh, him,' says the man, 'I saw him down yonder.' (I would know, of course, he's probably still living in that house fifty miles away in the county seat.) 'I saw him there a while back,' he says.

'He has taken up with a woman, they say.'

'That's the notion you get,' he says.

'How is he doing,' I ask, 'does he look well?'

'Doesn't seem too bad,' he says, 'he was cheery, and the woman was with him. You don't need to worry yourself about him. Do you think he'll come back, maybe him and the woman? You know him pretty well, don't you?'

'I do not know if he will come back,' I answer, 'I have no idea.'

The skinny man shrugs his shoulders indifferently. I

believe that in the course of time people have forgotten Tullipan and remember him only because I am still here.

The following months are cold and cloudy. It rains most of the time. I learn nothing more of Tullipan beyond a few rumours which I happen to overhear. He has recently been seen again, I hear once, in the county seat, he is still there, supposedly he was sitting in a café, gobbling some lunch ('gobbling and guzzling, I'm telling you!'). And I discover that he has been in trouble with the police. Vagrancy and such. Supposedly the woman is still with him or he is with her, who knows which. And apparently he is running around like a mad man, in his tennis shoes, undersized coats and shabby hats, with all his bags and trunks. And in addition now he is said to own a small donkey. He seems to be making a very jolly impression. He has moved out to a house on the point. The house probably belongs to the woman. And I am asked if he will ever return.

I answer that I do not know.

'Your guest! He ought to join the circus, just for the fun of it,' some people say, and laugh. 'He could romp around as a living ad for some camping equipment company.' 'Come on, now' says the shoemaker, 'all in all, I really liked that young fellow.' 'Oh,' says the postmistress, 'he wasn't much good for anything, it's too easy for people like him to lose their heads.'

I telephone the police in the county seat and discover that Tullipan had been in custody a short time for stealing. ('More like disturbing the peace and shoplifting food, you know, made off with the most worthless things,' says the officer over the phone, 'makes no sense to me . . .'). And they cannot throw him out of the house because it belongs to the woman . . . ('The house? out on the point, on the north highway, left, down past the paper factory, on by the frieght depot, through the underpass, then about half a mile down the dirt road . . .') He does not have any identification, he is unemployed, nobody knows who he is or where he comes from. 'His name? You mean what he's called?' The officer laughs: 'You don't know? He never wanted to give his name, crazy stubborness. He just laughed whenever anyone asked. Finally the woman said that his name was Pan, Tulli Pan.'

I vouch for him and say that he is related to me, and I tell a story explaining why he does not have any identification and where he is from, a tale as touching as it is plausible. 'Not a penny to his name,' says the officer, 'how is he supposed to live, on the woman's money? Me, I just don't understand . . .'

And I promise to pay a small sum, a delinquent fine. If anything happens to him, I say, you are to get in touch with me; I give my address and say that I can be reached anytime by telephone through the post office. I am to be consulted before any proceedings are started against him. And there is some complaining, but also the promise to leave him in peace.

One night I dream of Tullipan.

In my dream it is night and Tullipan appears in the doorway of the house and is about to go upstairs, and I hear him taking off his shoes, but I am awake and call out: 'Tullipan!'

'Oh, you're not asleep,' he says, comes into my room, and sits down in an easy chair. 'I thought you'd already be asleep, I wanted to be quiet, you know.'

'I haven't been able to sleep tonight,' I say, 'stay a while, if you are in the mood, Tullipan.'

'I don't want to bother you,' he says, 'I just want to fetch something. I need some stuff that's still here. I'll just go get it.'

'Go get it,' I say.

Tullipan goes up to his room, and I hear him moving about and talking to himself. He comes down after a while. Under his arm he is carrying the pictures that were hanging in his room.

'You know, I missed them,' he says and laughs, 'it struck me right off that I saw them nowhere else. Now I've got 'em back, knew all along they'd still be here.'

'How are you, Tullipan,' I ask, 'are you well?'

'Oh, I'm fine, you know,' he says, 'you fine, too?'

'I am doing fine,' I answer, 'when are you coming to get the rest of your things?'

'Those things? Oh, you know, I'd better leave them here; I don't think I can use them now. Have plenty of others.'

'The clock is still out there in front of the house,' I say, 'did you see it? An old owl moved into it last November and still lives there. A huge, blind old owl. She can sing songs and recite poems. She never has to be fed. I spend much time listening to her.'

'I didn't see her,' says Tullipan. 'I don't know anything about owls, you know. Show her to me!'

I get up and we go out in front of the house and I open the creaking, eerily whistling door of the housing and we see the huge owl sitting beneath the weights in the darkness of the clock cabinet.

'Oh, so that's an owl,' says Tullipan, 'she's beautiful, but she is so silent, too.'

'Shhh! Be very quiet,' I whisper. Tullipan stands motionless next to me, and we hear the voice of the owl, a muted, sleepy, singing sound:

> . . . take your hat off, mister,
> the wind's blowing warm today, mister,
> oh, slip your shoes off, mister,
> the wind's blowing warm today, mister,
> oh, take your hat off, mister,
> slip your shoes off, mister,
> another little cigar, mister?
> Oh, warm blows the wind today.

Tullipan nods and whispers to me: 'A beautiful singer and she's singing a beautiful poem.'

'She is singing so drowsily,' I say softly, 'we woke her.'

And we hear the owl begin again:

> Guardian Angel Cash,
> can I snare you so big
> with song and the dances
> of fate from your twig?
>
> I stand in the red
> and do what I shout:
> drink myself sick
> until I pass out.
>
> Guardian Angel Cash
> can I snare you so big
> with song and the dances
> of fate from your twig?

Here I am and I'll stay
and yell out my lungs,
what I do in a day,
is shown first by my tongue.

Guardian Angel Cash,
can I snare you so big
with song and the dances
of fate from your twig?

I can't wait to be lazy,
I'll have them on tick —
time lost, poems, hunger,
charge it all to Old Nick.

Guardian Angel Cash,
can I snare you so big
with song and the dances
of fate from your twig?

'Did you hear?' I say, closing the door of the clock cabinet.
'I think she knows by heart all the poems and songs in the
world. She has already sung Shakespeare's sonnets and even
the most obscure little ditties.'

'Does she know your things by heart, too?' asks Tullipan.
'You are always writing poems like that. People say you're a
writer and write such things.'

'She did recite one of my poems once,' I answer, 'I was
cleaning my bicycle and just happened to hear, oh, I stopped
and listened to her sing and found my poem so beautiful the
way she was doing it.'

'And you're still working so much, every day?' Tullipan
asks.

'Every day,' I say, 'whenever possible.'

'That's nice,' he says, then suddenly his eyes are flashing
close to me in the darkness. 'Do you know what,' he says, 'I
can fly now.' He laughs happily. 'Should I show you?'

'Show me how you can fly, Tullipan,' I say.

He climbs the porch steps in front of the door, throws
himself heavily into the air, swoops low over the front yard,
and, with little motion of his arms or legs, is lifted up, flies
higher and higher and disappears, small and dark in the
blackness above the roof top. I hear a loud roaring around the

house, a flapping and soft fluttering of cloth in the wind, after a while Tullipan reappears, floating on his belly in the air, as high as the eaves, he dives and in falling rights his body, he lands on the run and with quick bounds comes to my side.

'Damn, you really can fly,' I say, grabbing his arm in wonder. Tullipan laughs proudly and sits down on the steps.

'Shall I make some coffee, are you hungry?' I ask.

'No need,' he says, 'you know, I have to fly away again. I ate a lot of plums earlier. I don't need anything else, I'm flying off anyway, thanks.'

My dream ends here and I have awakened. It is early morning, the window is open and the cold air of February blows into the room. It is getting light and I hear the sea, a singular, distant sound coming from far off, surging melodically, fading into the heavens, dreams, or elsewhere.

In the time that follows I often meet Tullipan in dreams. Once I saw him riding offshore on a whale, waving. I happened to be standing on Meerstrasse repairing my bicycle, the front tyre was flat when I emerged from the shop, loaded with paper sacks and cans.

I heard my name being called (I remember now that Tullipan never spoke my name and perhaps never knew it) and I stood up, recognized Tullipan, and waved the tyre pump. The whale rushed by heading north, and on his back rode Tullipan, huge in his flowing bathrobe, and we waved until we lost sight of one another.

And once, in a dream which I remember, I see Tullipan in the mountains. I am standing at the edge of a wind-tossed wood filled with birdsong, out of it steps Tullipan, he approaches slowly and, so it seems, on tip-toes through tall grass, lays a finger to his mouth, steps up to me nodding his head and whispers: 'Be very still, don't move, listen.'

Silently, without stirring, we stand head to head, listening intently. And we hear a twittering sound close by.

'Do you hear that?' whispers Tullipan.

'I hear it clearly,' I say softly, 'what is it?'

'I have swallowed a bird,' says Tullipan, 'by accident. Opened my mouth maybe a bit too wide. Now he's singing in my belly. Do you hear that? He's been singing since he got in.' And Tullipan laughs loudly, shaking with pleasure. 'Oh,' he says, stopping short, 'I don't dare be so loud. I must be careful, with the bird inside. My belly shaking isn't good for him, is it?' 'If he can sing like that,' I say, 'then he can't be too delicate. And you do not have to worry about laughing.' 'Do you think he'll stay in my belly?' asks Tullipan. 'That I do not know,' I say, 'if he likes it there, then of course he will.' 'He does like it,' says Tullipan, 'listen to him sing!' And he laughs, bows, waves, and carefully moves off, stepping softly and slowly through the meadow, and disappears into the trees.

April has come again. My work goes more easily than ever before, and I write much. And whenever I meet anyone in the tavern, at the post office, in the shops, or on the wharf, there is no more talk of Tullipan. Other people have visited me in the meantime. They came by car and were nicely, properly dressed. We often ate supper at the tavern. And even they, those editors and writers from the city, friends and acquaintances from the immediate vicinity, and publishers and their assistants, were not unfamiliar with the story of Tullipan. They amused themselves with it whenever they could.

'You are just the kind of person to attract such types, don't be surprised if it happens again.'

'That is good material for a novel or novella,' they said, sitting around at night on the chairs in my study with books in their hands, talking and smoking, eating and drinking. 'You could make something really good out of that. Stop and think what you could do with a type like your Tullipan, or whatever his name is. You can have him turn everything inside out, or make a loudmouthed clown of him, you can have him chasing whores, gulping food, swilling liquor, you can practically have him run amok. God knows what he'd produce. A fabulous subject for you.'

'You should have used a tape recorder,' I am told, 'you'd have his entire tale by now.'

'You really ought to get to work on it and not write poems.

Everybody writes poetry. But novels are popular, especially the longer ones, and you should and you could . . .'

'Certainly,' I answered, 'that is fine for you, but not for me. All in all that is not such good material for me as you think. I do not want to make anything out of it that can be done so simply, and whatever you might imagine, a novella or the like, however you put your heads together, and whatever you have to say about it . . .'

'For me, there are a few catches,' I said. (Who among them really knew anything of Tullipan! Who had the faintest inkling of his origin, and whom would I have been willing to tell it to!)

'You are just too arrogant or too lazy,' said my visitors. 'Arrogant or lazy or not,' I said, 'I can't write about that, I simply cannot and will not write about that, especially about that.'

And again I see Tullipan in a dream.

He has changed into a giant. I see him rising up powerfully behind plains, darkened horizons, and great expanses of forest, his black shadow soaring across the heavens. His huge skull is streaked with red, his entire face distorted by wild, drunken laughter. He sees me standing somewhere along the edge of a lake, he waves to me, approaches with a few strides, beneath which there is the crunching and cracking of wood and stone, across the countryside, and stands broadly, powerfully over me.

'Tullipan devours everything,' he says with a laugh, 'and in the end, he will also swallow you. You, Tullipan will save until he is nearly full.'

Then he bends down and whispers so that my ears ring: 'Tullipan has an insane hunger, you know. One like you have never known.'

Against my will I look up at the belly hanging over me; Tullipan is fatter than I remember.

'Tullipan gobbles things up to make him full,' he whispers, 'it has to taste good!' And he raises himself up again and looks hungrily about.

'Look!' he says and with one hand rips a great forest from the mountain range, leaving naked rock behind in the distance. 'Tullipan eats it all!'

And I watch Tullipan swallow an enormous fist full of

wood and leaves and clinging earth.

'And that over there!' With his finger tips he plucks an entire farmstead from the meadow and stuffs it between his reaching lips.

And he gets down on his belly and before my eyes empties the lake with a few wild, smacking gulps. And he consumes the countryside, so that finally only I and some bushes are left, tiny and lost between his tennis shoes.

'And if you try to hide, I'll eat you up along with your cover,' bellows Tullipan from so high above me that echoes roll back and forth. And he bends down and takes me in his hand . . .

Once I saw Tullipan, lying on his back, drifting down a great river. This was also in a dream. He had placed a tortoise on his brown belly and was talking to it and it was answering him in a deep, bass voice. I was standing at the water beneath some tall trees and I waved to him and called his name: *Tullipan Tullipan!* Sluggishly he turned his head, but he did not recognize me.

The month of May came with blue colours and warm wind, middays came and went gently in white, and a long cool dusk preceded the nights. I again grew accustomed to working at open windows and moved my desk. A new volume of my poems had appeared, and I picked up a package of advance copies at the post office and sent them on to friends and acquaintances. I received a letter from Jennessy. (It had been addressed to the publisher and forwarded to me.) It contained a few words about my new volume that delighted me. I continued to work on my book and took a short trip abroad; it was the beginning of June when I returned.

A short time later, while I was working in broad daylight, a strong blast of air through the open window struck my face, throwing manuscript pages and sheets of notes from my desk, scattering them across the room. A large, rushing shadow was settling down in front of the house; and as my poetic papers sailed and rustled softly through the room, I stepped to the window and saw a helicopter landing in the front yard, its blades spinning light and shadow into gigantic circular patterns on the ground. Two persons climbed out, I

recognized Tullipan in the company of a short, bald, but trim
and distinguished looking man. Tullipan pointed to the
house, the man looked up quickly and followed Tullipan to
the front door. 'My God,' I thought, 'is someone coming to
bargain . . . to buy Tullipan from me?' I ran to the door,
opened it, and bumped into Tullipan.

'He is at home,' cried Tullipan, throwing his arms tightly
around my neck. 'I brought someone I think you'll like.'

Pushing the man before us, we went into my room. Hastily
I gathered pages of manuscript, laid them on the desk, and
set the typewriter on top.

'Where have you been, Tullipan?' I ask, 'so much time has
passed without you.'

'I picked up your friend, oh excuse me,' said the man and
bowed slightly, 'in the mountains. He was walking along,
carrying a rather large boat through the woods . . .'

'A little boat, you know,' Tullipan interrupts him.

'I approached him,' the man continued, 'introduced
myself and offered my help. Your friend set his boat down in
some ferns and informed me that he needed no help. He was
under way, looking for the continuation of a river that had
petered out right under him. He said he thought he would be
able to find the flow himself, I replied that most certainly no
water was to be found here, not even a trickle, whereupon he
left the boat behind in the fern thicket, explaining he would
continue on foot. I offered to accompany him, he was kind
enough to accept, and we went on together.'

'He stayed with me all the way,' says Tullipan, 'taking
twice the steps so he could keep up.'

'However that may be,' said the man, 'we came to a city on
a river, your friend believed he had met his stream again and
wanted right then and there to fetch his boat out of the
mountains, but he was not entirely certain if the water was
really the same, whereupon we decided to travel by rail.
Then I asked your friend, my companion here, where he
actually intended to go. He answered he wanted to visit a
friend. And so for a few days we went by train, by taxi and
tractor, and finally rented a helicopter because somewhere
along the way we had lost all sense of direction, but not the
desire to visit the friend of your friend, who, in all likelihood,
you yourself are. Flying back and forth in the sky we

searched and searched and just this morning found the sea, the village, the house, and finally you. And now here we are. My name,' the man bowed in introduction, 'is Jennessy.'

Full of joy I told him my name and we fell into each other's arms.

'Then you are the very person who is writing the book on Tullipan,' he said. 'And now I know that your friend and my dear, patient companion is himself this Tullipan.'

I nodded. 'How do you know,' I asked, 'that I would like to write something about Tullipan? I haven't even started to . . .'

'But, dear friend,' said Jennessy, 'everyone knows!'

'You're writing something, a book, on account of me?' asked Tullipan, pleased, 'specially about me, and am I in it?'

'Perhaps I'll write a book about you, Tullipan,' I said.

'Then I'll be in it twice, once like this and once in the book!' Tullipan laughed and rubbed his hands with glee. 'And what will I do in it?'

'You will do everything you always do,' I said. 'You will wear your tennis shoes. You'll laugh and drink and go walking in Meerstrasse. You'll hear flights of beautiful, invisible angels and hug a girl named Ulisanne . . .'

'I don't know her,' Tullipan interrupted me.

'You will stick a turnip in my nose to wake me in the morning, you will be friendly and peel cherries and plums as large as pumpkins for me whenever I am lying on the sofa with a strained, bruised spirit and battered dreams. You will lead the dear Lord himself to my desk and tell him he must at last read my books. You'll roast a little pig in the library, set fire to my Leather Stockings and my King Lear, you'll strike your crazy bone on a sharp ray of June sun and will be and remain the great, eternal, huge . . .'

'You've got to show me how I do all that,' says Tullipan earnestly.

'Show us all,' says Jennessy, 'and make our travel-weary souls rejoice.'

'But it is just a thought and not yet written down,' I say. 'for the moment I have something else, and it is just as good!' We go out to the front of the house and stand around the large, silent clock. I tap on the cabinet and say, 'Little owl, sing something for us!'

'There's a little owl inside,' Tullipan explains, 'she sings poems. That's a big job for a little owl. Between songs she sleeps and doesn't need food.'

'She sings and recites poems,' I say, 'I have heard her recite hundreds of them.'

'Does she know my verse from memory?' asks Jennessy.

'She probably knows every poem by heart, even the foreign ones. She speaks English and French, Portuguese, Spanish, and Russian, she speaks that quite well. Her mind is the mind of poetry, and so she probably knows your verse, too.'

'How is she started,' asks Jennessy, 'is she turned on or wound up?'

'Oh, she doesn't need to be wound up,' laughs Tullipan, 'she's a simple little old owl, natural enough. You can't tell her she is supposed to sing something special, she sings what she wants to.'

And as we are opening the door of the clock the better to hear, the voice of the owl begins:

> What can I do with my room?
> In it I put bushes and broom,
> fill it with clouds and with sea,
> but it is always half empty to me.
> I drive in some smoke and snow,
> before I see them they go.
> I catch up the storms and wind;
> thunder rolls out, not in,
> and I search for it sky and light
> and shadows, they don't fill it right.
> I, I bring in nice stones so tall,
> and you really can't tell it at all.
> Tired of the effort what's left I give
> to a passing swallow to fly off with.

'Do you know that poem,' whispers Jennessy, 'it is not one of mine.'

'Not mine, either,' I whisper in return, 'I don't recognize it. Quite possibly it is a translation. I have noticed that the little owl uses translations, and not always the best ones.'

And we hear the voice of the owl:

. . . oh of all
good things
a good end simply
to die –
light as a wind rose

And as I listen to these unfamiliar lines being sung, I do not understand why time and the light are changing around me. I hear sheets of rain hitting a roof and there is a thick darkness before my eyes. I feel about and touch a light switch, turn it, and find that I am lying on the sofa in my study. The typewriter sits on my desk, manuscript pages lie scattered on the floor. The open window lets in the cool night and pounding rain. I stand up and look about for Tullipan and Jennessy. There is no trace of them. 'If I do not find something in this room that shows they were here, then I have been tricked,' I think aloud. The house is filled with silence, I hear rain falling on the window sill, my papers, and my desk. 'And so, I have been tricked,' I think, close the window, and stand there in the room.

During the summer I have the wish to see Tullipan again. I can wait no longer and take the bus to the county seat, arriving near evening, and walk out the neck of land through growing darkness. An isolated house emerges before me after a while, wide and irregularly shaped with additions of rooms and gables. The doors and windows are open and filled with light. I move closer and see that the house is full of people and hear music, laughter, and women's voices. Two men are walking ahead of me on the path to the house, carrying a keg of beer between them, they enter and I hear them being welcomed, long and loud. I follow after them and stop at an open window. The people I see are all strangers and nowhere among them do I find Tullipan. The house appears to be sparsely furnished, I see only crates and old chairs, the walls are bare and a single, naked light bulb hangs from the ceiling of the room into which I am looking. And I see beer and schnaps being drunk, the party, or whatever is taking place here, cannot have been going on long, the people, young men and women in sweaters, work clothes, and colourful skirts, move about rather stiffly, quietly, and soberly through the room. I knock at the open window; a man standing nearby turns and leans out.

I say good evening and ask if there is a party.

'As you can see,' says the man, 'would you like to come in? Do come in.'

'That is not necessary,' I say, 'I was just passing by and wanted only to ask if I can speak to Tullipan. Could you call him to the window for a minute?'

'Hold on,' he says and waves into an adjoining room. 'Someone's here at the window for you.'

And someone else appears. I recognize him, it is Fridolin, he bends down a little and does not know me at first because I am standing in the darkness.

'Good evening, Fridolin,' I say, 'I just wanted to ask if I can talk to Tullipan . . .'

'Hello . . . the writer,' calls Fridolin, and I see joy on his red, sweat-covered face. 'Come in,' he says, 'Tullipan is not here, but come in.'

'Where is he then,' I ask, 'what is wrong with him, has something . . .'

'Come on in,' says Fridolin, 'don't worry, I'll tell you all about it, the door is there to the left.' I walk around the house, there is Fridolin, standing in the doorway, and he reaches out his hands. He is laughing, I think he is really glad to see me. 'How perfect that you are here,' he says.

'What is wrong with Tullipan,' I ask nervously, 'has something happened to him?'

'Nothing has happened to him,' says Fridolin, 'don't be upset. Here!' And he presses a water-glass full of schnaps into one of my hands and an open bottle of beer into the other.

And we drink and touch glasses and Fridolin says, 'Well, you know, he has gone away, he left about three weeks ago.'

'And probably no one knows where he is, is that right?'

'No, nobody knows,' says Fridolin, 'up to now nobody knows anything new about Tullipan.'

'And how did you come to be here,' I ask, 'and how are you, Fridolin?'

'We ran into one another when I was looking for work, you know, and I started coming by, and then he told me he was probably going to leave and that while he's away I was to take

over the house, lock, stock, and barrel. Well, and when I
came by, two, three weeks ago, Tullipan was gone, and that's
what I did, moved in. As far as I know, all of it is mine and
tonight we're having a housewarming, or something like
that, anyway we are having a party, and all these people here
more or less know Tullipan and are his friends.'

'Look,' he shouts into the house, 'here is the writer
Tullipan came from last year.' And with outstretched arms
he introduces me.

Everybody comes up and shakes my hand and pounds me
on the back and a fresh glass of schnaps is shoved into one
hand and a bottle of beer into the other, and they ask where I
am from ('Tullipan could never get it straight, you know'),
what I am doing and what my name is, if I came by bicycle,
train, taxi, on foot, or like a tramp, they ask me if I am
publishing anything, and if I had suspected that a party was
being given in the house tonight.

'Then Tullipan did talk of me?' I say.

'And how he talked!' is the answer. 'He went on and on
about the writer, again and again he told strange, new things
about you, quite fabulous stuff.'

Most likely, I think to myself, he has probably said that I
ride my bicycle on the sea, live in a clock cabinet, and eat
typewriter print for breakfast! In any case I am invited to stay
and celebrate, and I do stay, dancing and drinking all night,
talking, listening, making friends, and rambling drunkenly
through Tullipan's house.

In the first grey light of morning I take Fridolin aside and
ask him if it is true that Tullipan did talk of me. 'And he did
not forget me right off?' I ask.

'Why are you asking,' says Fridolin, 'don't you believe it?
He really must have liked you, because he talked about you
all the time, and about a few others who live down there he
must have known. I think he would have been happy, if
you'd come by when he was still here. To him you are a kind
of saint, you know, but for some reason he left your place, he
said.'

'Yes, he left out of anger,' I say.

'Now you are talking like a writer,' says Fridolin and
laughs at me happily. 'It couldn't have been all that bad. He
probably just got a little sore, you don't know him very well if

you took it so seriously. Just imagine the kinds of tantrums he has thrown around here, not to mention his crazy antics. Hours on end he used to stand out there on the cliffs, tossing stones into the sea, bellowing, while children were huddling up there on the railroad tracks, staring at him, scared out of their wits.'

'Did he spend much time with people?' I ask.

'Not much, except with us,' says Fridolin. 'He didn't bother with them, no, he really did not go out of his way. He was in pretty good standing and mostly they left him alone, sometimes they called him crazy and an idiot, but I don't think they ever said so to his face, or really bothered with him much.'

'Was Tullipan forced to leave,' I ask, 'perhaps because of the police, was there anything that made him sneak off?'

'No,' says Fridolin, 'he left on his own. One night.'

'And the donkey,' I ask, 'I heard something about it, what has become of the donkey?'

'Oh, it was found nearby on the beach, dead, drowned,' says Fridolin, 'an antique hunk of animal flesh it was. Tullipan left a short time later.'

'And the woman,' I ask, 'did you know her?'

'I knew her very well,' says Fridolin, 'she disappeared too.'

'Perhaps she ran off with Tullipan?' I ask.

'That's quite possible,' says Fridolin, 'she left at the same time, she very well could have gone off with him; he liked her and she did much for him, with the police and all, and the house was hers, but you could never tell, if you didn't know. Of course you'd think the house was Tullipan's. I'm nearly positive she is with him.'

'Were things going well for Tullipan at the end,' I ask, 'was he healthy, did he seem content, did he laugh much?'

'He was fine,' says Fridolin, 'he liked to stand near the sea or in the water singing songs, and making loud speeches nobody here understood. He drank much and laughed often and told his funny fairy tales, yes, he was probably very content toward the end . . .'

And in the early light, as I am trying to sleep, lying drunk in the sand not far from Tullipan's house (the party is still going on and I can hear laughter and music, and people are coming and going), I think of Tullipan and realize once more that he loves me. What does it matter, I think, whether he needs me; that is unimportant, he loves me and I love him and that is the way it should be.

Neither Fridolin nor I nor anyone else ever heard or saw anything of Tullipan again. Later I telephoned the police; they know he has left and Fridolin is now living in the house, but they are unable to tell me any more.

Often I ponder where Tullipan might be and try to imagine where he is living and how he is getting on. One thing is certain: Tullipan is alive. My creation cannot just disappear and die. What he has yearned for and gained with all of his might, he will keep for a lifetime.

I can be proud of Tullipan, but what am I to do beyond that? I am keeping company with a dream that overpowered me and then faded into its own background, a dream that has left a creation wandering through the twilight, a creation that in reality feels so close to life. That is a plain fact that does not seem so simple to me. Is there any proof that Tullipan ever lived in my house? I can lead anyone who inquires over to a few pounds of mysterious junk and introduce him to a few people who will certainly remember Tullipan, if I ask them about him. That is not much. And beyond that?

What happens if I ask: 'You remember him, don't you?' What happens if I ask about Tullipan and am left waiting for answers?

But I ask no one about Tullipan. I know better, I have no doubts. And if it were asked now: 'Who is Tullipan?' and the answer came back: 'Ho, that tall, broad fellow, that half-crazy fellow who used to run around here and then disappeared . . .'

Then I would rise up and say: 'That is my creation, Tullipan! He is my giant, my headman, my big brother.'

And if it were said: 'You have to prove it, what are you talking about, what do you mean by that, and what are you saying anyway . . .'

Then I would answer: 'I cannot prove it and it does not need to be proved. For Tullipan is my giant, my headman, my big brother . . .'

And if it were said: 'Why, you are just as crazy as that

giant, your Tullipan or whatever his name is; now just be quiet and don't talk so much . . .'

Then, without hesitating I would answer: 'Tullipan, it is he, my creation! He is my giant, my headman, my big brother!'

And one day in the fall I sit down at my desk and begin writing about Tullipan. I write all day and half the night, and the next morning I begin writing again. I write until I fall asleep.

In my dream Tullipan comes to the window, dressed as usual in a tall black hat and bathrobe and tennis shoes. He sticks his head into my room.

'Am I disturbing you,' he asks. 'I don't really want to come in.'

'No, you are not disturbing me,' I say, 'you never do, Tullipan, and I'm so glad that you have come.'

'You are glad, that's nice,' says Tullipan. 'I just wanted to ask, if you have time, we could take a walk, maybe, if you want, to the sea.'

'Come in, Tullipan,' I say, 'we'll drink some coffee and then walk down to the sea.'

Tullipan clambers in through the window, laughing, bearded, and huge.

'Then I'd better put the donkey in my room,' he says.

'Oh, you have the donkey with you,' I say, 'but I thought, Fridolin told me, your donkey drowned last year. I was certain he fell into the sea and I thought you had flown over here.'

'He is not dead,' says Tullipan, 'oh, he did once drown, but that is a far cry from being dead. If I can ride him, of course I don't fly. I rode over on him, there he is.'

And he points out his donkey, standing small, grey, and lazy in front of the house, turning its head toward us, indifferent or sleepy.

'Fine,' I say, 'bring him in, and we'll drink some coffee.'

Tullipan leads the donkey into the study and hitches him to my desk. And we make coffee and feed sugar cubes to the donkey. Then we race to the edge of the sea.

'Beautiful, the sea,' says Tullipan, stirring the water with his foot. 'It's already much colder.'

'Yes, fall is here again,' I say.

The sea fades away green and flat toward the horizon and the sky stretches endlessly, flashing with light, and we watch gulls flying high overhead and hear a cawing and singing from the beaks.

'You no longer live in the house,' I say, 'you have left and are somewhere else, aren't you?'

'I haven't been there in a long time,' says Tullipan, 'now I am someplace far away, my friends have the house now.'

'I know, I was there once,' I say, 'and I met all of your friends.'

'And I wasn't there,' asks Tullipan, 'are you certain I wasn't around, did you ask?'

'I did,' I say, 'and you were really not there. You had been gone two weeks, your friends were having a party and talking about you.'

We move along at the edge of the sea, spending hours together, we walk in the rolling water, but do not take off our shoes. The distant roar and spraying foam, the soft thunder, the sharp, wild smell overcomes us and we run into the sea and throw ourselves into the water and tumble laughing and coughing through foam filled with swirling white and brown sand, and Tullipan laughs his dark, loud laughter and beats at the waves with his fists, yodels, whistles, and shrieks with joy.

'Come farther out,' he shouts, 'can you swim?'

'Yes,' I call between two waves, 'I can. I am coming!'

And we work our way through the strong thrust of the green, cold water into the stronger surge of the darker and colder water far out beneath the sky. Then Tullipan suddenly leaps out of the sea, drawing behind him an ocean of flashing water drops, his huge body climbs, he is flying away, rapidly gaining altitude, flying in wide circles above me, calling:

'Farewell down there, I'm flying! I am flying off again, maybe I will come back!'

And Tullipan flies, scarcely moving his body, his arms and legs slightly unsteady, holding his hat in one hand, waving the other . . .

'But your donkey,' I shout as loudly as I can, 'don't forget your donkey, Tullipan!'

'You can k-e-e-p h-i-m,' calls Tullipan from above, waving and growing smaller, a dark disappearing point in the white glitter of the sky; he strikes out in a high arc over the sea and flies in the direction of the mountains.

And I struggle out of the water and stagger back on to the beach and collapse gasping in the sand.

And wake up —

And have awakened, without a doubt. Before me sits the typewriter, a half-written sheet of paper in it. I begin to laugh when I see the desk and the paper in the typewriter, Tullipan is written on it, Tullipan Tullipan. And stand up and step to the window. A brilliant autumn day is advancing warmly toward noon. I see the long lines of the mountains immersed in blue. And an old man is leading a donkey past my house and waves up to me.

'Ho, what are you doing with my donkey?' I call out.

The old man laughs and drives the donkey onward. And I stand at my window, wave, laugh, and make a deep bow.

Zünd

The baker in Milis has done a good deed, it would seem: he's
provided Zünd with a steady job. No other businessman in
Milis has ever done that. Zünd, unemployed from time
immemorial, has never had anything but odd jobs. He carries
luggage to the bus and stones to building sites, helps make
hay in the summer, transports cases of beer, and chops wood.
He's an equally transient and tenacious local figure, sitting in
taverns, lounging around at the bus stop, small-headed,
dull-eyed, mumbling and smiling, rarely communicative and
rather annoying. He inhabits a garden house that he can heat
and lock, at the end of an old cherry orchard. And Zünd took
over a new branch of the bakery a few weeks ago: he carries a
breadbox through the mountains.

The bakery in Milis owns two delivery trucks, which
provide the grocery stores, shops, and branch establishments
in the area with bread and cakes. That's an institution. It's
hard for the trucks to get up in the mountains; that hasn't
changed for years. Deep, shady sandy paths, with wide ruts
from wagons loaded with wood, frequently softened by
downpours, lead around bends up into distant mountain
valleys and end suddenly in forests and fallow swampland.
The gravel roads are under construction and in the meantime
shouldn't be driven on. The little villages are scattered and
remote, the grocery stores small and hardly worth regular
deliveries of cakes and bread. There are hamlets there with
their own baking ovens. So the baker can do no more than
send a bread-carrier up in the mountains. He called Zünd
into the bakery and negotiated with him over cigars. Zünd
agreed to everything, without even asking questions. He was
told exactly which road to take through the mountains. It
seems that he knows the area already; the names of the
villages were familiar to him. So the baker believes that Zünd
will do. An old breadbox was fetched from the attic, and

emuhl 1972   I/II

inside the lid a price list was fastened with thumbtacks. The baker himself printed it carefully by hand in India ink, thinking about the rain that might soak in.

Zünd knows what he's supposed to do. Before dawn he comes to the bakery and fills the breadbox with black and white bread, rolls, raisin bread, and little jam cakes. An hour before the delivery trucks set off he departs from Milis on the highway leading north. After a quarter of an hour he leaves the highway, crossing meadows of cherry trees that ascend to the level of the great forest. By then the sun is usually up; the early dawn makes forests and mountains recognizable. Zünd can see smoke from the bakery chimneys drift into the grey sky. He hears the delivery trucks starting off. Before him is the inside of the woods, full of bird-clamour and cool darkness. Now he climbs upwards through the woods. An hour passes. The light penetrates into the forest, uniform and brown, spreading itself out between the trunks. Taking a steep cut across root-covered narrow bends, he climbs on higher into the mountains. In a clearing the first sunbeam touches him. He notices it and stops a while or goes on uphill, the first stream of sun cool on his back. Around eight o'clock, if he has taken long even strides, he will reach the first groceries. They already expect him. He enters the store through the low wooden door with the bell over it, sets the breadbox on the counter, opens the breadbox, and waits. They take bread and rolls from the box, on Saturday a few jam cakes as well. Zünd points with short, horny fingers at the price list. The merchandise is reckoned up on the spot, and the cash is counted out on the counter before him. Zünd whisks it into his money-bag with the palms of his hands and smiles. They help him replace the breadbox on his back. He leaves the store and continues on his way; after two hours he has disposed of half the bread at houses, farms, and hamlets lying scattered higher and farther along the paths. Toward noon he has supplied three more stores. His box is lighter and rubs against his sweat-damp shoulders. He walks more slowly and more erect, and his feet have grown heavier. After one o'clock he reaches a little inn on the plateau, smiling, with his red-checked handkerchief damp in his hands. Here they know him already: he is coming to eat bacon, fried eggs, or potato soup. In addition he'll take a few rolls from his

breadbox; he has a right to, the baker said. He'll also want
coffee and some plum brandy; that goes on his own account,
the baker decided at the beginning. Here he usually stays for
an hour. On rainy days he sits in the dark parlour, which
smells of beer and smoke; on bright days on the gravel terrace
in the thick dark shade of huge chestnut trees. In the early
afternoon he disposes of the last of the bread in an out-of-the-
way shop and stows the money-bag in his hip pocket. The
rest of the day belongs to him. He'll take a different path back
to Milis, descending more slowly through less accessible
forest regions. Here and there he'll sit down on the edge of
the path, smiling and talking to himself. Lost in thought,
he'll scrape the dirt out from under his fingernails with little
pointed sticks. He may strike the breadbox against a large
rock on the side of the path. Then the crumbs and fragments
of crust will fall out; a small transparent flour cloud will fly
through the fern and sink down on leaves, needles, and
stones. He washes his feet in a water-hole, shakes sand and
stones out of his shoes, throws them in the breadbox, and sets
out again barefoot. He carries the empty breadbox through
some places that don't buy his bread, for they buy other
bread from other bakeries or have their own. At twilight, on
many days even later, Zünd will come back onto the highway
south of Milis and go immediately to the bakery, before
which the delivery trucks are already stopped. He gives the
baker or manager the full money-bag and sets the breadbox
down next to the cash register in the store or, if it has rained,
leans it against the warm black oven. He packs a few rolls in
his pocket — he's been promised them — and leaves the
store. He goes home in the darkness. Sometimes he drinks a
few glasses of beer in a tavern that lies on the way, usually
alone. During the night he is lost from sight.

For several months Zünd has performed this work to the
satisfaction of the baker. September has come. On the
plateau rests a full golden lustre, the inside of the forest is dry
and cool, in the orchards apples, pears, and plums are being
harvested. One morning in that season Zünd comes to the
bakery as usual, fills the breadbox, and leaves the store.
Everything else is uncertain. The only thing certain is that
the groceries Zünd usually reaches between eight and nine in
the morning wait for him today, wait for him in vain, wait for

him in vain until afternoon and then no longer. All other
shops, groceries, houses, and farms wait at the usual time for
Zünd and his bread, wait in vain until afternoon or evening
and then no more. Today nothing is seen of Zünd, his bread,
or his breadbox in any of the places through which he's
supposed to come. It wasn't bad weather that kept him from
bringing the bread, they reflect here and there, for it's a
perfect September day. They don't call the bakery in Milis
right away, either, for an oversight or something of the sort
can happen, and so they count firmly on Zünd for the
following day. Finally, around midnight of the same day, the
people in the bakery become worried. One of the delivery
men is sent out to look for Zünd at home. The garden house is
locked, and nothing is stirring. It seems that Zünd is not at
home, and the delivery man comes back unsuccessful. In the
taverns they're saying that Zünd disappeared in the
mountains. Someone says it was only to be expected. A shop
on the route is called after midnight. Zünd hasn't been seen
here, they are told. All night long a light burns in the bakery,
in case Zünd comes back at night. And the baker has the
annoying thought that he has wound up with the wrong
bread-carrier.

And now where is Zünd loitering about? Invisibly the
story has followed the bread-carrier, as only it can do. A
will-o'-the-wisp of forgotten, down-at-the-heels poetry, a
nameless story with the name Zünd, it clings to him even off
his route. Only through the story can we learn about Zünd. If
a narrator were at its disposal, it would read as follows:
Zünd? He's left the highway now. He's taking the usual path
through the cherry-tree meadows. He enters the woods. It's
dark, and he leaves the route without meaning to do so,
cutting across the woods without thinking that he could have
lost his way. It's still early in the day. Cool and moist, the
morning air touches his skin. He stuffs his cap into the box
with the bread and looks around. In his head, so it seems, is
no thought of bread or grocery stores; he's lost them in other,
older woods. Behind the trees and high above them a huge
blueness comes up. It's *that* sort of day, thinks Zünd, I can
tell it right off. It's that kind of light, the kind that comes into
the day as it starts. White clouds are lying around in the sky.
Zünd sees them later on too, when the day is already quite

full of the light, and he opens his eyes and lays his head back. Far out over the forest, higher than the trees, white clouds, this is what Zünd thinks and sees. And he strays even farther from the path; that happens, it seems, while he's looking around, and when one eye and then another lights on stones, woodpiles, and white clouds. Zünd watches the tips of his own shoes walking. Once he sets down the breadbox, unbolts it, looks in, presses his nose against the bread, and takes the bread out, counting it piece by piece on to the ground in the forest. He counts it back piece by piece into the breadbox breadbox. He may even take a small loaf aside, crush it toothless and slowly, and swallow it quickly. That tastes good, thinks a sense of well-being in his mouth. That's a kind of brown cloud in my stomach, thinks Zünd. White cloud, think Zünd's eyes. Breadbox breadbox wood, thinks Zünd's back. I'll fly the bread around in the forest for a bit, thinks the breadbox breadbox. Strange feet are getting to know us, think the untrodden paths in the forest. Wind mild, heavenly child, think the trees standing windless on the mountain. A Zünd is carrying a breadbox into the world, think the trodden, untrodden paths on the mountain.

Now it seems that a huge, light, special cloud is going through Zünd. A wild little storm of joy rains all the way out to his hair and toenails; unaccustomed, a little thunderstorm of joy. Satan's Saviour, thinks a joyful Zünd, giggling. It's running headlong through Zünd and throughout him. It's making the palms of his hands hot and moist, so that he, Zünd, has to stand still and lick them off. That tickles, thinks a small giggling in his breathless agitated head, which is dripping with sweat and moving back and forth as he walks. That pulls your shoes off your feet, think Zünd's moist hands, so that more such joy comes to Zünd. Then the leaves and needles trail so much new joy over his feet. Satan's Saviour, groans Zünd, delighted. Too much joy, too many such little storms. A person can stand in a brook and let it wash away, thinks Zünd. A person can also take water in his mouth, he thinks, can wash bread and bread. Zünd washes the loaves, washes raisin bread and rolls, washes little cakes and breadbox breadbox. A person can also walk along carrying breadbox breadbox. That's forest, a day full of trees, thinks Zünd. The trees are for running through, for staying among, for shadow-catching and breadbox breadbox carrying. They're for mountain hiding, thinks Zünd slyly. And a person can go on, he can even throw away his shoes. Satan's Saviour, he can breadbox breadbox. He can be Zünd and carry breadbox breadbox. But that brings me near people, thinks Zünd. There the groceries are hungry for bread from Zünd, so that the bread in the breadbox breadbox leaps. Where there are no groceries, a person can set down the breadbox, rub his back on the tree-trunk, rub the breadbox, rub his hands against the breadbox, so that the breadbox wakes up, the bread in the breadbox wakes up. So that Zünd can give it one of his little storms of joy. Bread, raisin bread, a person can call, thinks the mouth, and that's how Zünd hears it. Bread, raisin bread, Satan's Saviour, so it seems. We're being hawked, thinks the bread. A person can also go on go on, thinks Zünd, bolt the breadbox again, think his hands. Because bread is not being sold, everyone is already full, has enough rolls, has enough bakers. The breadbox comes back up on Zünd. The joy is compressed into a flat cake of sweat on his back. The bread is carried through forest and forest, through many times more than one forest, until new groceries are on the path and the rolls turn somersaults. A head-shaking comes from strange groceries, so it seems; Zünd and breadbox breadbox are sent away. Zünd bows before the breadless trees, so it seems. And it saddens him suddenly that he can't lick all this burdensome joy off his feet. But he can lick his joyful hands. What use would shoes be in keeping off all that joy, think the feet. A person can go on carrying the bread, thinks Zünd. There's Breadbox-Zünd, thinks the white cloud, thinks the sky, thinks Zünd that the sky thinks. I'm a breadbox, thinks the joy. Satan's Saviour, thinks Zünd, and licks his hands. I'm leading a Zünd through great forests, thinks the story . . .

In the afternoon Zünd sets the breadbox down on the edge of a white sandy path. He's exhausted, and all that weary joyfulness sticks and tickles on his sweat-damp skin, runs slowly and nauseatingly through his body, and settles noisily and painfully in his head. His green shirt shows a dark sweat stain, which has made a damp spot on the back of the breadbox. He unbolts the breadbox and counts the loaves, scatters white sand over the loaves, and smiles. Following the sandy path, he comes to thick woods and makes his way in. His bare feet are stung by the rank-growing nettles; he laughs, startled, and his toes clench. On a grassy area he stops and empties the breadbox out on the ground, in front of his feet. It seems that the sight of the bread lying around makes him furious. Still holding the breadbox over his head, he stands there, his eyes narrowed in excitement. After a while his locked knees buckle. His face becomes thoughtful. He throws the breadbox into the bushes, crouches among the loaves scattered in the grass, and starts eating, slowly, mechanically. Soon he gulps down the bites, hurriedly and carelessly. When night comes he looks for the loaves still scattered in the grass. He gropes through the grass with cupped hands, crawling on all fours. Groaning, he stuffs the loaves fiercely into his mouth. A little later he falls asleep, tossing restlessly. In the night he vomits repeatedly and writhes through the woods, knocking half-asleep against branches and tree trunks. Near morning he falls into a heavy and stupefied sleep, lying on his stomach.

The next morning he wakes up and doesn't quite know what to do with himself. He seems to remember having carried a breadbox, yesterday or today or some other time, for he begins groping and rummaging around in the grass. He finds the breadbox later in a stinging nettle bush, packs it impatiently on his back, and works his way out of the woods into the open air. Reaching a lane, he follows it without hesitation. Later, setting down the breadbox for a moment, he notices that the doors are clapping to and fro and the breadbox is empty. He shakes his head and reflects. Discomfort seems to overpower him, and unclear, fleeting dread. His face twists into vague, suddenly changing grimaces. He goes on and reaches a forest at noon. There he comes upon a clear brook rushing over dark golden leaf mould. As he washes his head and feet, he discovers a frog in the damp leaves at the edge of the brook. He picks it up carefully and sets it in the breadbox. When the frog leaps out, he catches it quickly again in the black leaves and kills it by flinging it repeatedly against a stone. He takes the dead frog, sets it in the breadbox, bolts the breadbox doors, and goes along the brook, smiling and unhurried. In the towns he goes through this afternoon he opens the breadbox and points at the dead frog.

It may be an accident that later he winds up in a shop on his usual route. His behaviour shows that he doesn't recognize anyone, and his wares really make them wonder about him. They ask him for black bread and white bread, rolls and cakes; he points at the dead frog, his mouth open, laughing and urgently nodding. They keep him there, offer a cigarette. Without touching the frog, they put the breadbox aside. And while the shopkeeper and congregated customers make conversation with him, someone telephones the bakery in Milis from the hall of the shop. They advise detaining him in a friendly manner and promise to send a couple of men as soon as possible. The shop has filled within a few minutes. Zünd is exuberant and seems to be telling a story, which everyone pretends to understand, whether straightfaced or laughing. Now they notice that Zünd arrived without shoes. Zünd is smiling and mumbling and licking his dirty hands. In an hour and a half a delivery truck from the bakery drives up. The two delivery men and a police assistant from Milis enter the store. In the next room they're shown the breadbox and the dead frog. The police assistant, an older man, throws the frog out the kitchen window, as someone suggests. The delivery men, whom Zünd fails to recognize, take the smiling one between them and tell him to climb into the back of the truck. Meanwhile they talk about Zünd in the shop. He must not have wanted to fit in, they say. Why? He must not have had a good relationship with his Lord God, or he with him. Why? He must have been one of those loners, they say. The police assistant carries the breadbox out of the shop and shoves it into the truck behind Zünd. Before twenty or thirty spectators the truck drives off toward Milis.

Zünd no longer goes through the mountains. The baker has had him taken away; apparently it's been arranged that Zünd won't come back. His garden house has been cleaned out and rented. Zünd may live for a while yet where he is now, or he may not. At the present no one brings bread into the mountains. There they have almost forgotten Zünd, and the breadbox breadbox too.

The Crow

I was crossing the woods in the summer; they were dense woods that had no end. And one morning I met a man with a tattered jacket and dirty boots who was standing in the brush. He shouted and whistled through his fingers (that's how I noticed him), calling many names again and again into the endless woods full of murmuring and mating, rustling and green silence. As I came near, he beckoned to me and said he was seeking a tiger.

There were no large animals or predators in these woods; but I didn't let that stop me, for I had curiosity enough and plenty of time. I had him tell me the names and helped the man look for the tiger. I went through bushes and tall, sharp grass, calling the tiger's name here and there in the lull. I heard the man working his way through the thicket far ahead, whistling and shouting. After a long period of useless searching in the woods I met him again, and he said: Now we must look for a bear, for I saw a bear running over the wooded hills, and that means the tiger has transformed himself. There is no more tiger.

And we set out again into the woods, went our separate ways and called all the names of the bear into the vast twilight, and I heard groping and rustling, wood crackling and heavy steps on leaf and stone, near and far. When I met the man again in the black inmost centre of the woods, he said: I saw a white elephant go through the bushes; there is no more bear.

And we parted again and fought our way through forest and more forest, endless and cool, called many names and looked for the elephant and did not find it. And after several hours the man said: From now on we must look for a wolf, and we looked for the wolf. In the afternoon I found the man sitting exhausted on a tree stump, and he said: I saw the wolf transform itself before my eyes. Now we must look for a black fox. With branches and sticks we prodded the sandpits and hollows around the roots of trees, prodded into the impenetrable thickets and islands in ponds. I scrambled up a tree, sat high above the ground in the forest, looked far out over the woods and into the sky flooded with light, climbed down again, crept over the moss and through the fields of fern, but I found no black fox.

What shall I do with the fox if I find it, I asked the man. You must call me, he said; you must hold it until I come. So I set off into the forests once more, now very tired, and near evening in the brush I came upon a crow the size of a man, standing motionless. I stopped running and asked: Is it you who is being hunted here, crow?

The crow nodded and hobbled toward me.

Does the man already know that you are a crow, I asked; has he already seen you? No, said the crow. He is still looking for the black fox. The crow seemed very tired.

I am helping him search, I said. You know that, don't you?

Yes, I know, said the crow. I saw you run past me when I was a bear, catching my breath behind a heap of stones.

You could easily have torn me to pieces, I said.

Yes, said the crow. I could easily have done that, but I didn't much want to. Even now I could hack you to pieces, if you don't prevent me by thrusting your stick in my beak, or something like that, but it doesn't much matter.

I didn't know what to do with the animal. I said: If you like, I won't tell the man that I met you as a crow. You can stay here; I will keep the man at a distance. I don't really know what's going on here at all. You can rest a bit, but you must stay awake. I'll come back.

The crow shifted its weight to the other foot.

What will the man do with you when he finds you, I asked. What does he have in mind?

Chain me up or put me in a cage, answered the crow. I am just guessing. I don't know exactly. He could also kill me and eat me; it depends on what occurs to him when he finds me in the form of a crow.

Does he have any right to you, I asked. I mean, did he build you a handsome cage when you were a tiger, did he feed you?

He hunted me even before I was a tiger, said the crow. He's a great hunter.

I asked the crow: Do you intend to transform yourself again, crow?

It answered: I can do it once more, only one more time.

All right, I said, I shall let the man go on looking for the black fox. And I went through the woods, found the man hoarse from shouting and tired, and we agreed to continue the search for the fox.

I have hunted the tiger and all the animals before him, said the man. I have hunted the bear and the elephant; now I am hunting the fox. I am a hunter, this is my living, and I need the beast, I want to possess it. And if it should perch on the towers of Peking as a parrot I would hunt it down.

What do you plan to do with it, I asked.

What will I do with it? That's quite irrelevant, cried the man impatiently. I must have it, I want to possess it; and now go and look for the fox.

We parted. And while the hunter was roaring in the woods for the black fox, I hurried to the crow. I was not possessed by the desire to have the crow for myself. It was still standing in the same spot. Will you come with me, I asked it. I like you; you would not be hunted any more . . .

The crow looked at me and nodded its big head. We walked along now, the crow reeling with sleep at my side, looking for the way out of the woods. We found it late in the evening, when the twilight had already made the forest grow dark, and we went out on to the plain.

The hunter will not leave the woods, I said. Here you can rest.

And the crow lay down in the grass. I laid my head under the wings of the crow, and all night we slept in the plains near the woods. From the woods came muttering and shouting, and the next day we rose and went on together.

And we went on through the hot day that shone on the plains. On the edge of the flatlands the woods disappeared, small and grey. The grass around us was sparse and stirred in the wind. And after hours of crossing the plain I asked the crow to fly up and see where we were.

I can't fly, said the crow.

I asked the crow to try, at least. The crow flapped its wings, flailed about with them, hopped. It turned around clumsily, drew in its feet, dragged its wings on the ground so that a cloud of dust rose, and nothing resulted but a few short, awkward leaps. The crow's breath rattled and its eyes were wild.

No, you really can't fly, I said, so never mind. And we went on in the immense heat. Hours later we came to a village. We rested in the shadows of its trees and washed ourselves at a trough. The crow jumped into the water after I had drunk, flapped its wings, shook itself, sprayed water about, sucked water up through its beak with great loud gulps. Many people gathered in the doorways and around the trough, pointed at the crow and laughed, surrounded it rudely, but the crow did not notice or paid no attention. I told the people that I was taking the animal to a circus in the city. I expect to get a lot of money, I said. After a short time we left the village (the people made way for the crow with reluctance) and I apologized to the crow. Don't misunderstand me, crow, I said. I needed an excuse for the people.

I knew that already, said the crow. It didn't really seem embarrassed.

And we went on across the plains, came through low hills, until it was afternoon. I'd like to make a suggestion, I said. You do have another transformation left, don't you? That's what you said.

Yes, said the crow. Why do you want to know?

What sort is it, I continued, is it a conspicuous one?

Is it absolutely necessary for you to know? asked the crow.

Look, crow, I said, here's a suggestion. Listen to it. We'll be coming through many villages now, sometimes into cities. There will be many people, a thousand and more in a day, you see. It would be simpler if you would transform yourself once more, if that would make you less conspicuous.

Why, asked the crow. I am a crow. Anyone can let himself be seen with a crow.

That is true, I said, but have you ever seen a real crow?

No, said the crow. I know very little about crows. I have learned from you for the first time that I am a crow and am called crow.

That's just it, I said. Real crows are small. 'You're thirty times, perhaps forty times as large as an ordinary crow. And you're the only crow who has ever been so large. So you'll never pass for a crow. As a dog, for example, you would hardly be noticed, for there are hundreds of kinds of dogs, very large, very small. But there is only one kind of crow; everyone knows that.

The crow walked along next to me and brooded for a long time. I don't quite understand you, it said. I want to save my last transformation, you see, because it's the last one. I used to change quickly and thoughtlessly. Now I must think for a long time before I give anything up. That's one reason. The other is: why shouldn't I go on being a crow? I like being a crow, as I liked being an elephant, for instance, and only reluctantly became a wolf after the elephant. I would like most of all to remain a crow, even in the cities through which you say we will come.

You could be hunted again, I said.

I hadn't thought about that, said the crow.

But it would be good to think about it, I said. We spent the night in a hut near a river. At night rain fell; it beat gently on the tin roof of the hut. And in the morning the crow said to me: You must not misunderstand me. I have my pride even as a crow. I would like to remain a crow, even if we come to a city in which the people are not used to such big crows. I shall remain a crow.

All right, I said, you will remain a crow. If I could, I would force you to transform yourself, but I can't. And your pride gives me pleasure, too. — For a few days we went downstream through grass and plains.

Later we came to a city. It was early fall and the nights had grown cool. I led the crow over the boulevards and wide streets. It had never yet been in a city, but did not seem very confused; it walked along beside me with clear, calm eyes. On the first evening they threw stones at us; the crow winced. We were soon encircled by a mob, were driven faster and faster through the streets. Soon I was seized by them.

I don't know this town, crow, I said, as the people closed in. I don't know where you could hide.

The crow stayed near me, silent and uneasy.

Transform yourself now, I said, as the people pushed me away. Transform yourself, quickly!

No, said the crow. I saw it begin to tremble. Its wingtips twitched. The crow tried to flap its wings. Already many stones were flying at the crow. Its beak was wide open.

Change, I shouted. Go on, change!

But the crow hopped clumsily on down the street. The crowd fell back as far as it could. More and more people followed the crow, faster and faster, and more and more stones pattered onto the crow, who swayed and reeled under the blows.

Now the crow looked around for me, searching with its wild, helpless little eyes, until it found me in the crowd. Then it transformed itself. That went very slowly. The crow stretched painfully. Black crow feathers swirled around over the crowd, which shrank back in horror and clustered together. The crow transformed itself silently. Its skin swelled in and out; then it was finished. A giant blind black cat stood alone facing the crowd with wet, empty eye-sockets and ruffled fur, to which crow feathers clung. It spat in loud, hoarse blasts. It didn't move from the spot, only groped around a little on the ground with its paws.

Now I understood the crow better. The people started throwing stones at the cat again, more and more stones. The cat turned around and around in the same place, spitting, until it fell down. Stones and crow feathers still flew about. The crowd had released me long since. And I ran away through the strange town.

Gulliver's Death

'It seems I used to eat more oats, didn't I?'

'Didn't I?' he shouts in his cracked voice, his earlobes quiver, peevishly he peers over his shoulder into the room and listens for an answer, but none comes. Bits of furniture swim past his gaze, chairs, vases, and ocean maps in the grey atmosphere, nothing else in the house moves. He can hear himself breathing, the gurgle of some spit in his throat.

His armchair has been placed by the window, the old man has been left alone. They know he likes to spend his afternoons at the window, doing nothing, a rug across his knees. They have put a small table within reach, there's a bell on it, and a cup of tea that has gone cold. They respect his wish to be alone, and besides, that is the best way to deal with him. He used to travel in earlier days, this gentleman, his travel reports were famed, he had them published and everywhere, even in Oxford and London, people used to talk about him and about his prose with astonishment, suspicion, respect, and sometimes in a tone that never should have come to the old man's ears. Dr Hogard, his personal physician and longstanding friend, called it blasphemy against Christian reason. Even just a few years ago there was much coming and going of visitors, scholars, mariners, men of letters and members of this or that academy — he made no bones about throwing them out of the house. Waiting on the stairs the visitors could hear Gulliver's high-pitched voice bleating and giving orders for the riffraff to be driven away, with dogs if need be. For some time now he has been left in peace, and the days are quiet. That is as he wants it. Now he has time enough to occupy himself with his own person and his memories. Usually he spends the morning behind closed stable doors with his stallion, Clamys. Left to his own devices, he's as patient as a sheep. True, his disgust with humans has become more noticeable than ever. His tone is coarse, his answers, instructions and demands lack all tact. The sight of people makes him feel sick. At the least provocation he has a screaming fit and he stares at people as if they were rats. So people avoid his presence, even his wife only sees him when the doctor pays a call. James, the groom, is his one connection. So darkness may fall without Gulliver having touched the bell. Night is a circumstance that pleases him. The scent of rain and horse dung floats through the window, which is kept open a crack, day and night, to admit fresh air. Gulliver sits in the unheated room, it is December, and a damp gust of wind brushes over his sunken face. Sounds from outside, a footstep, the grinding of coach wheels, a door banging from over where the groom lives, are all beneficially remote, belong to the stillness of the night, have nothing to do with humans. The wind is rising. He likes to listen to it.

Occasionally his old weakness for reasoning comes over him. He picks excitedly at the threads of the chair and shakes his head. Did God really want us to eat white bread and drink tea? Wasn't it originally intended that man should be a horse, and therefore eat oats and lap water? Wasn't it originally intended that the human voice should be the whinnying of a horse, proudly and beautifully praising the glory of being created? Wasn't earth meant only for the Houyhnhnms? Gulliver gives a wry smile and clamps his toothless jaw shut. What a horrible joke, that I should be clever, but evidently not clever enough, and so little capable of forgetting myself and my creator, in whose ridiculous image I'm supposed to be created? People have told me I don't love humans and have never done so, never even loved myself. What's that supposed to mean? A reproof? Don't make me laugh: not loving humans, what do I care. I've clung to my contempt. That alone made it possible for me to become unlike humans, these ones around here. But — what have I become, and whom do I resemble more than myself? And what am I? Ridiculous. His shapely fist knocks against the table, the bell tinkles faintly, the tea spills. This whole performance! Dr Hogard. And he keeps on coming back, although time and again I've thrown him out. Tea and valerian, he says. Tea and valerian and every other conceivable device to prolong this life a while. Yahoo! And me? Thoughtfully he rubs his back against the chair and peers across at the teacup. The question remains: Did I use to eat more oats than I do now?

Thoughtfully — but nowadays he's not often so disposed. Usually he sits quietly in his chair and thinks he is a Houyhnhnm. When he sits quite still and no sounds distract him, his illusion is complete. His eyes focus on a point somewhere on the wall, or they drift, fixed and expressionless, through the rain and winter twilight outside the window. He is a white horse and dreaming of oats and straw. Or he moves, led on a halter by James, toward a point in the darkness where Houyhnhnms — he can see them — are on parade waiting for him. They will lead him into their palaces, so that he can be, perhaps forever, their guest, sharing in their conversations. Those are the happy moments of his old age. And the stillness of the night favours this dream of his, which he dreams with open palms and a sagging jaw.

After midnight James comes into the room. He crosses it soundlessly and touches his master's arm. Gulliver gives a start, jerks his head to the side. His elbow jabs James in the hip, but the smell on him of stables and horse-sweat calms Gulliver and he subsides into the chair.

'Yahoo, have you brought some oats?'

'Oats, sir?'

'Didn't I tell you to bring me some oats?'

'You must go to bed, sir,' says James, 'it's almost one o'clock.'

'To bed, to bed,' Gulliver parrots him, 'take me to Clamys.'

'That's not the thing, sir,' says James. 'You must go to bed, you must sleep.'

'Do as I tell you, Yahoo, and help me up.'

James lights a candle, helps Gulliver out of his chair and leads him down the stairs. Going to the horse at night, that's new, James thinks; oats, I don't know what he wants oats for. Let him eat them, for all I care, and choke himself.

'Stay here, sir, I'll bring your overcoat.'

Small and thin, Gulliver stands by the door of his house. Behind him the light of the candle flits across the wall and dabs over the darkness in the corners of the hallway. He gropes for the doorpost and props himself against it. He inhales the cold rainy air, in short breaths, through mouth and nose. The spaces between outbuildings lie gloomily before him. His legs are shaking. That's because of sitting so long, he thinks, no oats to eat, only tea and white bread.

'Your overcoat, sir.'

Taking small steps, supported by James, the old man scurries across the yard. The candleflame, angled sideways by the night wind, gives a faint light. The silhouette of a coach looms up, backed by the plank wall of the pigsty. Trees, sinister barren branches beyond the roofs, the sky dirty grey behind them, the wind in them, roaring. The wind plucks at wet leaves that cling to the ground. It throws a few plump raindrops into his face.

'A puddle, sir.'

Gulliver sloshes ill-temperedly straight through the stagnant water. Bedroom slippers, wet, idiot, Yahoo! It doesn't harm my old hoofs.

In the stable there's a vaporous warmth and the glorious scent of Clamys. The stallion steps heavily to one side and lets Gulliver approach him. He pats the warm, firm neck of the animal and strokes his skin. James places the candle on a stool. 'When should I come to fetch you, sir?'

'Go to bed,' says Gulliver, 'I'll be staying, till, hm, I'll be staying . . .' He rubs his nose impatiently. 'What are you waiting for, I can get myself to bed.'

'That's not the thing, sir,' says James, 'I should come and fetch you, it's night time.'

'Yahoo,' says Gulliver, and swallows some spit, 'what's this, are you contradicting me?'

'I'm not contradicting you,' James replies. 'Where do you want me to put the stool?'

'I'll put it where I want it myself.'

'Goodnight, sir.'

The candle flickers, behind James the stable door has closed. Suspiciously Gulliver listens to the groom's retreating footsteps. The straw rustles. 'Clamys,' he says softly, and pats the stallion on the neck, 'now where had we got to when we were interrupted?'

He places the candle on the brick floor and pulls the stool into the trampled straw beside Clamys. Slowly, spreading his legs, he lowers himself on to it. The hem of his overcoat brushes across the black horse-apples.

'Where did you say we'd got to?'

'I know, I know,' says Gulliver, 'you don't like these conversations. What? They tire you out. To talk is a horrible weakness, if one talks like a Yahoo. Enough, we'll do no talking today.'

'Listen,' says Gulliver, after a while; he listens, strenuously, his earlobes quiver, he turns his face toward the stable door and fingers his belt buckle.

'Can you hear that?'

'You can't hear anything . . .'

'You can't hear anything,' says Gulliver, satisfied. 'We can't hear anything. No footsteps, no screaming, no idiocies; nothing that could remind us of them. They're asleep.'

Gulliver leans forward and wags his jaw from side to side. The wind beats in gusts against the stable wall and roars in the roof.

'They're asleep,' says Gulliver, 'how nice. But in a few hours everything will have gone to hell again. They'll wake up and wallow like pigs, they'll be grunting, running around, doing this and that, you know them. They make sure they're alive and take care that nothing and nobody slips away from their line of business. What monstrous displays of boredom and folly! How vulgar the racket of it all! Kicking up a stink and doing business, day in day out. Horrible. I have to guzzle white bread, and you pull the coach. But now everything is quiet and they're peaceful as rabbits after feeding time. I've come to eat oats.'

'Why do I want to eat oats?'

He rises from the stool, stands unsteadily and makes a vague lunge in the direction of the trough. The horse's tail sweeps across his face. Gulliver sways, his legs buckle, his bony behind falls back hard on the stool. The candle flickers and chases the shadows from their positions, across the brick wall.

'You shouldn't do that, Clamys, you should let me eat oats, shouldn't you?'

He stoops, topples over and falls on his hands. The stool capsizes. Slowly Gulliver crawls through underneath the stallion, spit trickles from the corners of his mouth and drips on his hands, his earlobes are quivering, sweat appears under his wispy hair, he stops crawling and wipes it away with his fingers. These humans! They've confused Clamys entirely, they've confused me too. What's going on? Doesn't he recognize me? Of course he does, he recognizes me, knows who I am. Hm. Oats. He doesn't want that. Why? As if I was, was . . .

'Why I want to eat oats? You're asking, asking why I . . .' Gulliver shakes his head.

'Tea and white bread! How could I be a human, captain of several ships? That's what the doctor wants. I tell him: I don't want it. Terrible. Enough, enough — these humans are wrong to feed me with white bread.'

Gulliver licks the spit from the corners of his mouth, groans, and pulls himself up by the stallion's left foreleg. He pats Clamys on his moist mouth. The stallion restlessly jerks his head aside and tries to back away from Gulliver. Gulliver falls head first into the straw. He shakes himself and places himself on all fours beside Clamys. A soundless laugh. Where had we got to? Gulliver bows his head and kisses the left forefoot of Clamys; the stallion shivers.

After a time, Gulliver stands up, props himself against the horse's body and tries to reach the trough. His outstretched hand manages to seize some oats. He stuffs the oats, trembling with greed, into his mouth; his jaws grind. He goes down on his hands and knees, crawls slowly around the horse, straw and horsedung are sticking to his overcoat. Just as he is on his knees and about to set the stool up, Clamys gives him a kick on the head. Gulliver falls across the stool, rolls aside into the straw, and lies there.

Still shivering, Clamys lowers his head, plunges his mouth deep in the trough and stands motionless, not eating.

Gulliver, captain to his majesty the lord of the Houyhnhnms, is boarding the royal ship. A horsehead is his figurehead, and the sails are made of brown Yahoo skins. Gulliver gallops across the gleaming deck and casts his gaze upon the calm sea. The servants of the king, two sorrel stallions, bow to him and fling wide the wing doors to the royal cabin. Gulliver enters and bows to the king. The king nods and invites him to be seated. The sea is calm, says Gulliver, we have oats and water for at least seven years on board, if your majesty would like to give the command to set forth. The king nods amiably and Gulliver bows. We shall now travel, says the king in a pleasantly resonant voice, as he studies the faces of the Houyhnhnms surrounding him, to the land of the humans. How shall we be received, captain? The humans, your majesty, Gulliver replies, are entirely capable of upsetting you and giving you grievous trouble. If you fear misfortune, turn away from this voyage. The king slowly shakes his head and replies: We shall be friendly with them. I do not doubt that you will treat with courtesy even the vilest of scoundrels, answers Gulliver, but I have told you, your majesty, in the lands you'll be entering, reason and toleration are unknown. We estimate, says the king with a smile, that in due time all living beings will bow to one another, do we not? Gulliver makes his obeisance and goes on deck, to give orders for the ship to get under way. The weather is clear and the expanses of the sea shimmer in the brilliance of the rising sun.

In the morning James enters the stable. Clamys is standing with his head hung low. Beside him, doubled up, Gulliver is lying. The stool is overturned, the candle has burned down, its wax spilled over the floor. Gulliver's face and hands are covered with dried blood. Oats hang from his half-open mouth.

An Unpleasant Story

I received a telegram saying that I had won a valuable and distinguished art-prize: the award was to be made in Berlin, my presence was absolutely necessary, also as a pre-condition for my receiving the prize I had to bring all my possessions and display them personally. In spite of this condition I accepted the offer and travelled to Berlin.

The award took place in the auditorium of a public building. Enormous applause began as I walked on to the stage and bowed. A speaker, who was unknown to me, made a laudatory address, he spoke for an hour or more, but nobody could understand what he was saying, because uninterrupted applause drowned his speech. Finally he made his bow, pointed to me with an expansive gesture, retired amidst roaring applause, and I was alone on the stage.

All my possessions had been brought to the place in a small truck. (I didn't have many things), and now, one by one, they were deposited on the stage. I walked forward, held them up, each in turn, showing each thing on all sides: books, editions of the classics, bottles of turpentine and nitric acid, overcoats, socks, metal-cutters and a teapot, cylinders, knives, wooden sticks and copperplate printing paper, a typewriter, a blanket, a few bottles of old wine, also letters, photographs, and manuscripts. The applause was so enormous, increasing with every object I showed, that I made gestures to dampen it, and used the microphone to ask people if they would be a little more restrained. This request only made it worse, and all my movements, a smile, head-shaking, shrugging, picking an object up or setting it down, only increased the applause still more. A gigantic room full of clapping, stamping and yelling, gaping mouths and heads wagging with senseless rapture, a humming, clucking, whistling, banging, roaring — I stuck my tongue out, thumbed my nose, bared my teeth, spat, flung books, crayons, tubes of paint into the auditorium, and turned my back on the crowd; the applause increased still more and finally assumed such hair-raising proportions that I gathered up all my possessions, put them one by one behind the curtain, and, with the applause still increasing left the scene.

As the tumult of applause roared and swelled behind me, now without reason or orientation, enormous and deadly, I ran down the dim corridors behind the stage looking for an exit. I saw that my possessions were lying strewn all over the corridors (workmen who had earlier helped me had now disappeared), books dropped, tools flung down, papers trampled on, crumpled, and torn, clothes and pictures thrown on to heaps of swept-up paper decorations; I asked people who were passing by — spokesmen, councillors, jurymen and suchlike — to help me collect my things, but they neither helped nor gave any answer. While I was picking up the remnants of my possessions as best I could and taking them out of the building, a group of men appeared in the exit (or entrance), in their midst someone was moving, supported under the arms, and being pushed and tugged forward in the direction of the auditorium, and did not seem to be able to move with any will of his own, his legs dangled weakly crossing the floor, and a group of workmen followed, carrying boxes full of objects, books mainly, drinking-glasses, a spinet, pictures, clothes and bundled manuscripts, evidently the possessions of a new prize-winner. For a moment I saw the drooping head, the face of a man, almost covered by a white collar, an uncommonly pale and blank face, and I recognized that it was a poet who was a friend of mine and who had recently died. I left the building as quickly as possible, stood beside my possessions on the pavement, and looked around for a taxi.

It was some time before one came and stopped for me. The driver helped me to pack the remnants of my possessions into the taxi. It was a cold, shining afternoon in October, my clothes were soiled and torn. I crawled into the taxi and lit a cigarette, the driver promised to take me to the airport.

Oswald 1972   Glockenspiel für Natascha   19/25

Workshop Notes:
The whole world and a few drawing pens

The several hundred etchings I have made were produced on an old 8 cwt press (origin unknown: surface 100cm x 50cm; roll diameter 30cm) and a small modern copperplate press which can fit into the back seat of a car, and which I have provisionally screwed to a crate stuffed with odds and ends. The heavy press used to stand in the laundry room in Freiburg where I made my first etchings. Now it is in Oetlingen (South Baden) in the house of my friend Ernst Vogel, bachelor and globe-trotter. The light press is in a little house in the country near Suzette (Vaucluse, France).[1]

I have no studio of my own and no properly equipped workshop. So I work wherever I can find space enough, preferably in junk rooms and cellars full of rejected wardrobes, watering cans, and fruit cases. I like used things better than things unused and new; so I prefer to work with the old press, rather than with the new one. The best work room I ever had was a junk room on a ground floor, with fruit trees outside the window; my best work table was an old door supported by trestles.

Having no workshop of my own, I have to make do with whatever equipment is to hand. In Oetlingen I use a small and very impractical electric heater for warming the printing plates, in Berlin a gas cooker, in Suzette a stove which smokes horribly, fuelled with whatever wood I can find lying around behind the house (dead trees, old telephone poles).

I have lost many of my plates or have carelessly left them to oxidize in damp cellars. I make only small editions, pulling ten sheets at the most. I print my own sheets, because I know my own plates best and am convinced that the best of printers could not print my plates better than I can.

I buy my copperplate paper from Radecke's in Hamburg;

my zinc plates (copper would cost too much) I buy from various hardware stores in Berlin-Kreuzberg, cutting them with my own shears. Black japan, copperplate paints and varnish I buy at Wicke's, in Berlin-Tempelhof. Turpentine and nitric acid I buy at the nearest pharmacy. My favourite pharmacies are rundown country places which smell of lavender essence. The lacquer base for the zinc plates I make myself, from an old eighteenth-century recipe. The recipe was given me by a very good Munich printer on condition that I kept it secret. The lacquer I can make is better than any other I have tried. Cobbler's pitch and venetian oil are also used for the printing.

My etching needles are ordinary drawing pens; for felt I use my typewriter pad.

Working ten hours at a stretch one sweats a great deal, so it is pleasant to drink while working. Tea with brandy in it, beer or wine; wine is best. Wine from the barrel, bought at the Ox Hotel in Oetlingen; bottles of wine from the hooper's at Binzen (Baden) — quality stuff, litre bottles, mature wines — and red wine from vintners in Provence. Beer from corner bars in Berlin, or cold canned American beer; wine whenever possible; it tastes best when you drink it with the prudence of a Black Forest countryman.

It is pleasant to print early in the morning or at night with the owl hooting from the tree outside your window, or with moths fluttering in through the open window and settling on the damp sheets that smell of turpentine. It is pleasant to hear music while you work — in winter time, say, when the window stays closed — blues and ragtime classics, records I fished out of the sidewalk boxes of English and French music shops: 'O Down by the Levee', and 'Skokiaan'. It is pleasant, while working, to smoke a few cigarettes and look at the freshly printed sheets in a good light.

2

Wine barrels, drinkers, eaters, dark herons in the Bowery, and cognac faces exhaling steam on a cold winter day on Coney Island, wrapped in green sea mist. Gangs, hoods, and white society waistcoats; a rundown Mona Lisa, or Angel Baby's sabbath face with hat and lipstick; highways, bus stops, boulevards in the morning, wind and desert, Oakland

Bridge against the white evening sky, and dockside sheds in
Genoa; straw from dolls, samovars, candles, mice, and men;
cities and suburbs, canons, graveyards, cherry trees—I draw
them all.

Night and day I am on the road through landscapes
familiar and unknown, seen and imagined. There I have met
beings I do not know and which I am at once compelled to
catch, that is, to draw: so that they shall belong to me, so that
I can become conversant with them. Foreign creatures,
apparitions with coppery dog teeth and mailed forearms,
they keep bringing other creatures along with them,
sometimes they astonish me, overwhelm me, creatures that
are mysterious, in a way, seeming to dwell closer to the heart
of creation than myself. They bring with them troops of
huntsmen and trappers, complete hunting parties with
packs of dogs, horses, and provisions; now come scoundrels
with boxes, pistols, and uniforms, very wicked street-
acrobats dancing on one leg and brandishing tattered Chinese
lanterns. New people, places, and objects appear, gradually
define themselves, I don't yet know what places and times
they come from, I don't know them and must make certain of
them at once with pencil, ink, and a sharp dependable
etching needle.

And down I go into the strange inexhaustibly expanding
landscapes; as I draw, I make my track through them, at first
a single track, and, while drawing still, I am settling myself
down in my whereabouts. Here I maintain myself, must of
necessity do so, inside my diminutive, wobbling, one-man
encampment, and yes, I can make some useable annotations.
Open-eyed I move on, slowly, laboriously or frivolously,
time is passing; and one day perhaps I shall strike against a
limit: there is a bar of fog, an uncrossable edge of the magic
world, whose first and only forest ranger I am; so I turn
around, go back to my point of departure, equip an
expedition, work through my notes, provide myself with
hundredweight packages of copperplate paper, handmade
paper and notepads, needles and pens, black japan, and
turpentine; I make sure of arriving as quickly as possible at
my work table and etching press, saw up wood for the
diabolically crackling, smoke-spitting stove on which the
etching plates will be treated to take the colours, and I work

until I have perfect prints before me: the first results, first booty of my expedition.

I go on drawing and hear nothing but the scratching of the pen on the zinc, and finally I can interrupt my expedition, a set of etchings is complete, there is no more to be done. The draughtsman is promoted to Horseman of Lake Constance,[2] and the sixty or eighty sheets are lying between two covers on the table, a pile of dry and ordered papers. There they are. They are there. The draughtsman ought now really to be content, so people think. With a hungover face he scrabbles around with his papers for a while, occasionally looking at this sheet or that, hardly his own any more, and then he begins a new work.

Translator's notes

1 In 1970, Meckel moved from Suzette to another house, near Remuzat (Drome), for seven summers. Ernst Vogel died in 1970.

2 Refers to the legend which tells of a horseman in a hurry who dropped dead with astonishment on seeing that he had just galloped across the lake on horseback without noticing it.

Felicitation for a Painter's Calendar

On a summer morning she lies on her blue blanket and considers what she'll do today.

She has woken up feeling as she did during the heydays of her childhood, as if, more or less, she had slept on the wind; she knows the story of the princess and the pea, but this morning she is one up, she has been sleeping on a plume of the Golden Bird. Her hands are light, her dream has gone, retained by sleep. Already the light is there, behind the curtain, and the dusty white morning of one of the dog days brings to her the word happiness, a word she can make use of. She has woken early, her eyes are open, but the word stays with her, seems to belong to her, for a while, this morning or longer, it stays with her because she does not speak it, and perhaps she does not even claim to possess it.

While the wind puffs the curtain into the room or pulls it out through the window into the light, she can hear, for reasons the day conceals from her, the sound of corn sacks being hauled across the floor, a sound she heard twenty or thirty years ago, on a holiday morning in East Prussia, when she awoke, and the horses had already been watered and her countless Polish relatives were drinking coffee in the kitchen of the farmhouse on the hill of wheat, round and huge and yellow as it was, or still is. She also hears, for another reason that only the morning knows, or the night that is past, the train running behind the huts in smoky East Berlin allotments, and the two-hundredweight footsteps of her father on his way to his coffee business. And she hears the wind which now, this morning, actually, is tugging at the tattered trees in the hollows behind the house. But perhaps she hears nothing, quite simply nothing. Or anyway almost nothing: the complete stillness, full of light and bees, of a summer morning in the mountains.

While the kettle is on for tea, she puts the basket chair

Chirico 1973   2/25

outside on the overgrown terrace, at the precise spot from which she can see the mountain and across the other way, and a bit lower down, to the rocks which on rainy days assume the dark tea colour and in the evenings are silver foil. There are some poppies and broom near the chair, whitened wild oats near the dead cherry tree, further off the rough hewn stone wall of the ruined tavern building, which adjoins the farmhouse, and the birds' nesting holes, visible between the rounded broken tiles. Directly below the weedy terrace the road passes, hardly wider than a footpath, and little used. On some mornings the farmer from the nearby farm comes past with his horse and cart, the last horsedrawn cart in this neighbourhood, and she sees the small dog with bells on his collar, between the wheels, and the old man with his moustache and sullen alcoholic face. Further down she can see, in front of the district attorney's summer house, the silver poplars, dusty white when the wind turns their leaves, but quite motionless this morning, a dull green. Still further down is the village, and behind it the plain, far off and vague in the morning mist, therefore good for sending thoughts into, for the searching out of things she would like to see, because they are absent.

For a time, nothing happens. She is there, the morning does not move; dull white steam from the teacup threads its way into the light. She has time to take a look at the light, the mountain loaded with clouds, or clear, the birds flitting in their straight lines, the vineyards above the road and the illumination, each day different, of the landscape, a changing illumination that she likes especially in September, when indolent powdery days come and it is a pity if you spend them indoors.

She supposes that, a bit later in the morning, the baker will drive around the curve below the house, singing at the top of his voice in his delivery truck full of currant rolls and cartons of biscuits that are never sold; and she thinks it is fine to know a few things about people she has hardly met, to know, for one thing, that the attorney conducts, with acrimony and perplexity, a constant battle against the mice in his house, because they eat his blankets up.

Now she'll go into the house and do something. There they are: the weeds at the doorstep, the long staircase with its dusty stairs, a handrail from nineteen hundred, the books, lexicons, and newspapers on the landing. At the top, to the right, her room — the light, softened by the curtain, is resting on her desk. The sheets of paper are there, the piles of picture frames, large and small, which she has collected in the course of time in a variety of antique shops and Berlin junk shops. On the stool, the heap of watercolours begun but not finished, the open-lidded Greek chest where she stores her own paintings, the Mexican rug and the wooden comb that came from Tlaxcala, the little blue and white spice rack (stamps in SALT and pen nibs in MARJORAM), the old wardrobe belonging to the house, with the musical boxes on top, mirrors and little wooden painted boxes; there too is the bundle of lavender, so dry it is almost black, a water jar from L'Isle-sur-Sorgue, half full of cognac, four or five liqueur glasses that go with it, and a copper bell with a scratched wooden handle. By the window, the multitude of brushes, water pots, paint bowls, watercolour cases, and, a little further away from the window, bookshelves stuffed full of books, and on the walls her latest watercolours in worm-eaten frames, some of them gilded.

From her desk she can see part of the cracked basin of the swimming pool, overgrown with ivy, and the grass path leading from road to house, and she can see the tall chestnut trees behind the farmhouse, she gazes across the plain below in the southern distance. Now she'll start to paint, but first she'll write letters, because the mail truck will soon be here, she can hear it now, mounting slowly the curve of the stony road; it honks when it stops at the houses some distance away in the hills; it first becomes visible at the farmhouse, a patch of yellow among the chestnut trees, then it drives up the grass path, turns among the weeds and stops, its engine still running. She would like to receive every day a big bundle of various mail, copies of signed books, letters from friends in Munich, Berlin, Brazil, and the little country of Vaduz, and unexpected good news from people unknown to her, who know her paintings. In any case the newspaper arrives, to bring the morning to a close and put off the start of work. She sits in the shade of the house wall, at the big table which stands on wooden blocks in the grass, it is hot now, the light immense; she reads letters and the paper — news, which supports not at all her word happiness (she never asked for it); she reads an announcement saying that Paustovski has died; she has read his books and it meant something to her that he should be alive — and now this brief announcement. His death preoccupies her, she would like to talk about it. The day becomes brighter and older, the heat even more intense, and still she hasn't started her work.

She is thinking now that she'll work all day, but not so as to make her back hurt or her eyes tired. So, while freshly painted sheets of paper are drying on the windowsill (weighted with stones because the wind is blowing), she'll go for a walk behind the house, on the narrow path through the trees, perhaps, where in June the cuckoos call; that is where the hammock hangs, the broom is fading there now, it is where the wilderness begins, with fallen trees and great lizard rocks. She'll eat a melon, look for cigarettes, perhaps thumb through old Brehm's animal lexicon looking for a heffalump that is never to be found anywhere else, or she'll remember a bit of Robert Walser's prose and want to read it again, immediately; she brings out the book about Chekhov, because she read in it once that there must be 'something more sensible than happiness'.

In the entrance to the house she finds a dead moth, the wind has blown sand and dry twigs across the doorstep. Her idea of what to do next is vague, for working hours at her desk are all identical, only the light changes, it moves over the papers that are spread out and illuminates with stripes the oval miniatures hung on the door. Time evaporates, visible behind her and before her eyes. She is painting a very small picture, has been at work on it since yesterday, and is still uncertain whether she can bring it off. She may be painting several pictures at the same time. While a picture is drying in the sun, she starts work again on an older one at which she has been brushing and sponging for months on end — but what is it that she is painting here, what is it that she really does? The pictures and colours look, one might think, like the sort of thing somebody might do on a holiday, and why is the background of her pictures always so tenebrous, so unexpected? And the figures which populate her pictures and look as if she had painted them with her left hand: what about these merry characters shaken out of a coat sleeve, tilted birds of paradise, old gaffers with canes and pipes, Brother Blot the chimney-sweep, one-legged dancing twerps and landscapes with funeral tapers wandering around in them, narrow and dark toy houses for horrified lantern children who stand on one leg and hold high their lamps? What is it she has brought into the visible world here, what is she doing with the world, and who needs her pictures, who is there to love coloured paper umbrellas for houseless otterfaced happiness, who to love a bumblebee garden, headstands and laughter, a shack for the sun that walks on two feet, fruit trees, when the dark comes early in chequered October, and rain falling into hay across the Fischingen hill?

In the afternoon she will interrupt her work, her back is hurting and her eyes are tired now. She washes her brushes and, whether the painting is finished or not, she places under a glass frame the paper that watercolouring has rippled, so that she can examine it closely, and so that it will be pressed flat. The evening is still to come, but it is early yet, the light still bright, only just after six, the sun is going down on the wide mountain ridge beyond the cuckoo's trees, so she stays sitting there a while longer. She can drive now to the town six miles away, go shopping in the small dark stores and drink tea under plane trees in the café on the square, watch the fat-bellied farmers arriving from the villages in their vehicles, and the schoolchildren rambling home.

Then the mountain night comes with owl and wind and total darkness. She switches on the light downstairs and in the various rooms, moths flutter against the windowpanes, dogs bark in the farmyard. Darkness brings people and conversation into the house, it opens books and breathes a melon-scented stillness. Now one can drink wine, celebrate, and pass the time. The peace is wonderful. There are cicadas, too, only now does she hear them, although they have been screeching all day. It is night, and time is vanishing, but she has no thought of that, for the day has only just begun and more than noontime and happiness is in store for her.

The Negro's Story

I tell you, I was a hunter and hunted alone. I had my own tracks through the forest and didn't share anything with anyone. I tell you, often I left home without a word, I vanished for a few days and nights and heard people saying: He's looking for his snake, looking for his monkey. I tell you, too: there was a panther living in the forest. The panther was older than people's memory and he couldn't be killed. It was certainly so, bullets couldn't pierce him, I tell you, he ran through every fire and crept, not so you'd notice, out of every trap. I tell you: a panther. There were good hunters who had seen him, and others who thought they'd seen him, and there were very good hunters who were certain their bullets had hurt him so badly that he'd slipped into hiding forever. But nobody had brought the panther out of the forest, not even one hair of his beard, not even a bone. Nor me, either.

I'd let twenty years pass by, telling myself: There can't be a thing alive that a good hunter who's patient can't kill one day, or hurt badly. I tell you, a panther isn't immortal, and I tell you: it's not patience I lack. One day I noticed I was getting older. So I wasn't going to wait any more, I got ready. I took my bedroll, rifle, ammunition, knife, matches, salt, and some bread. I didn't say goodbye to anybody. I tell you: my people will have seen one morning that I'd vanished with my things. Now I took the tracks I'd hacked out earlier and I used other hunters' tracks and got far into the forest, no trouble. I was strong and didn't get tired easily and soon I came to places where the bush was scattered and the thickets spaced out between swamps and streams. I spent nights in the windless hollows and clearings. I shot birds and cooked their meat in the evenings and slept by small fires that would burn out by daybreak. I tell you, I searched the forest many days without catching sight of the panther.

I got to be impatient but I didn't give up. I was tired from sleeping so lightly by the fire, but I wasn't fussing about myself any more than I needed, to keep my strength up. I'd been patient for a long time when one morning I saw the panther close to me in the underbrush, a big animal he was, and old, with his flesh hanging loose, and a lot of scars in the skin of his head. I took aim carefully, fired several shots, and waited for the panther to spin round and drop dead in his death-leap, but the panther wasn't hurt and he ran off. I followed him through the bush and the panther kept on stopping the same distance ahead of me. At noon on this day I got very tired and had a hard time keeping the panther in sight. Just when I'd stop a moment to get my strength back, I'd notice that the panther had stopped too, and was waiting for me a little way off. That surprised me and I was certain I'd kill the panther very soon. But before night came I was so tired that I lay down and slept. I tell you, the tiredness was stronger than my will was, so I lay down.

Once the panther noticed I wasn't following him any more he turned back, searched me out, and saw I was asleep. I tell you, he walked around me, nudged me, and in the end he lay down right there beside me. All night the panther lay beside me in the underbrush and watched over my sleep. He only went away as I woke up, toward daybreak. I noticed my sleep hadn't freshened me, yet I got up and was determined to go looking for the panther again.

Looking around, I saw the panther. I tell you, the panther was standing nearby and looking at me. He began to move, seemed to be running faster than ever, and I fired several shots at him, no result. I tell you, the panther still wasn't hurt. At noon my tiredness came back and after a few more hours it was so strong that I lay down and slept. The panther turned back, lay down beside me, and waited for me to finish sleeping.

For many days and nights this happened and I got to be more and more exhausted; one morning I couldn't get up any more. I lay with my eyes open in a heap of leaves and cursed my exhaustion, cursed the panther, who was lying beside me and looking at me. Finish me off, I said to the panther, you can see I can't get up any more. But the panther stayed there beside me and looked at me. And I said: What are you waiting for? I'll never get you; I never knew I'd get to be so exhausted. The panther, he didn't move. He lay there and waited and looked at me.

I tell you, morning and evening he walked round me, licked away my sweat and tried to help me out. But I couldn't stand up any more. What if I'd killed you? I said. The panther didn't answer, nor did he move away. After three days of this, I died. Then the panther jumped up and tore me to pieces. He tore me apart, in rage and despair. I tell you, he tossed my bones through the bush, and he roared. He roared for many days and nights and my people heard the lamentation in his roaring and they knew I was dead.

Tunifer's Memories

*— sometimes I catch my vague mind
circling with a glazed eye
for a name without a face, or a face
without a name —*

1

Tunifer's memories, therefore mine. Yet I've never been able to make quite certain that they're really mine. They might be someone else's, bundles of false impersonal memories, perhaps I've housed them, as well as may be, which is not well at all, in my past, which in the course of time (but what does that mean — IN THE COURSE OF TIME?) has fused into a makeshift past. Time past, makeshift image of things, my ragbag full of everyone else's stuff, my load of junk. Memories without established copyright. And me, lording it over untravelled winter days that creep in on me or flit away, voices of women, featureless houses. Glimpses into other people's perplexities. Indiscretions which I never desired and which consequently give me no pleasure, no support. If it weren't for Tunifer's being perched in this perilous way on obscure memories, he would be more free in his dealings with the world.

'Memories lying around inside me like stones tossed into a well.'

To the point, no doubt, but what should I do with them, having only the mind that does the remembering. How to tell which are false and which are true, superfluous memories and necessary ones. How to put the unprovable memories out of action. How to block the holes through which alien lives trickle into my mind, and through which my own life escapes, relentlessly. How to catch the rustlers and counterfeiters inhabiting my memory.

— and I remember a morning in that birdmad, wildly green, swampily hot Spring, when we were living, just ourselves, in a bungalow. We sat in the kitchen, and through the tight mesh of the insect screen, which for some reason had been oiled, we watched the humming birds among the elm trees. Lora (or Ana or Julia) had fastened a bottle full of honey water to a branch, neck downward and with a device enabling the hummingbirds to drink with their beaks. We were sitting at the kitchen table over the remains of breakfast (we had long and good breakfasts that Spring), and we gazed into the light filtering through the screen, the light of morning, still cool, and heard and watched the tiny bodies of the birds crisscrossing in gay confusion and the swaying horizontal surface of the water in the bottle as its level slowly sank, and which would disappear during the morning through the neck of the bottle, and Julia (or Ana or Lora) showed me how the long beaks penetrated the bottle top, and we saw the bottle swinging on strings among the leaves whenever a humming-bird pushed away and whizzed off or hung with whizzing wings in the air, guarding the bottle, and we sat at the table until the light fell among the gathered plates, and I remember — no, I don't remember. I remember the silence of that morning, the stillness of the light, unless I'm confusing it with the light of a different morning in another place, and I remember a cockroach that ran around the kitchen walls later that morning and knocked against an empty wine bottle, but I don't remember if Lora's name was Ana or Julia. I couldn't say whether I slept with her or not, or what colour her eyes were, or what shape her breasts were and in what language we spoke to one another and how long we lived in the bungalow that Spring (if it was Spring, and if it was a bungalow). And although there's so little to be said that's definite, I cannot give it up, that morning in the kitchen. I want to keep it, although it's not complete. I want to hold on to it, because it seems to consist only of itself and can't be connected with anything else or be affected by anything else. No matter how real, how alien, or how much my own it is — I want to speak of it, even if it means that I have to invent someone else's girl friend for my own use.

3

—and I was living in an apartment house on the Boulevard Martinique, but seldom spent any time in my apartment. Too much was happening that winter, parties in villas, clubs and dance cellars, every other evening I was standing around at some party or other, I drank and talked too much, waited for taxis at house entrances, slept in strange houses, agreed to meet people I couldn't have cared less about, wasted time, had a girl friend who was interested in music, so that I spent three evenings out of four in plush seats at boring concerts, though I understand nothing about music and was unable to learn anything about it during the eight or ten weeks of that attachment (Schubert's dying of syphilis was the only thing that stuck in my mind). I slept till late in the day, then telephoned for newspapers and tea, listened to Joan's noises in the bathroom (I say JOAN, but this name doesn't seem to match the face I remember or think I remember), spent the afternoons in cafés, discussed Wittgenstein as everyone else was doing (I've never read him) and Sartre too (no interest for me, none), a life of lust, boredom, negation, effortless and without particular appetite, without particular inner or outer ravages, and without loneliness, whatever that is. And I remember that night when I (Tunifer! Tunifer!) came home with Joan, worn out by an unusually loud Prokofiev symphony. Someone was leaning against the door of my apartment, he seemed exhausted and was blocking the keyhole. I said hello, waited for an answer, finally asked him to move, and recognized a fellow from that season's café and party clique, the sweat-damp and oddly puffy—how shall I describe it, obliterated— face of a popular friend and crazy dancer who had died and been buried a few months ago in southern Mexico. There could be no mistake. I was trembling with fright. Anxious moments, then terror, speechlessness. I retreated a few paces and pushed Joan aside (she probably thought he was a drunk). The man's mouth opened. Unbearable slowness of his lip movements, a dried-out lifeless hole—Pluto's lips when he asks for food— incoherent noises took shape, not human, could actually be heard, were pushed out of the mouth by a furry tongue, while sweat ran to the man's chin and trickled down his neck. Finally I thought I heard my name in connection with the question: could he stay with me overnight? Now I noticed his clothes, a worn-out leather overcoat, wet over-trousers too large for him, a buttonless army shirt, and sodden sandals (it was a night of driving snow and cold). I pushed past him, opened the door, tried to avoid touching the slack body, held Joan back, ignored her protests, waited until slowly, unbearably slowly, as if he were moving under water, he had staggered ahead on dragging feet and slumped into an armchair, followed him into the apartment, while Joan stomped past me and shut herself in the bathroom, sat myself on the edge of the table without taking off my overcoat, looked at him, came under the gaze of his bulging eyeballs, or more correctly, fish eyes, which were fixed on me, as if he were expecting from me some guarantee of his being alive. I replied, against my will, THAT HE COULD STAY, OF COURSE HE COULD, and he stayed there, where he sat, or hung, in the armchair, didn't move, his eyelids slid down over his whitish eyes and wetness ran from his clothes, making marks on the floor around his sandals and the chair legs.

The next morning Joan had vanished. I don't remember how and if we spent the night together, the two of us, the three of us (I saw her one more time at a party and have never been to another concert). The man stood in the room and looked at me. His clothes had dried into wrinkles. He asked me to give him money for a taxi, since he now wanted to GO HOME. He held out a slip of paper with an address on the east side of Alamandango written on it (whose handwriting?). I pulled myself together, held him under the armpits and got him into the elevator and out of the building, thrust him into a taxi, gave the driver the slip of paper and money, gazed after the disappearing taxi, thought for a while, came to no conclusions, remembered party conversations (shifting weight from one leg to the other, superior carpets, incoherent dialogues) in which he had been spoken of as someone WHO HAD BEEN IN but now had died somewhere, retired, so to speak, from the club, top hood of another season, someone to talk about, nothing more, and I began to realize that he was now back again, perhaps not completely, perhaps only halfway back, but still present, visibly, tangibly, and unavoidably claiming a place in my thoughts, destroying firmly entrenched memories, and I realized that it wouldn't be easy to accomodate him among the living or the dead, in the past or the present.

The next day the telephone rang. A stereotype DO YOU KNOW WHAT'S HAPPENED? forestalled my questions, and I heard that this person, who had appeared (dead? half dead? living by compulsion? what a monster —) had already been knocking at several doors and had been sent away, or hadn't been recognized. That he was being excluded. That he had broken out of his grave in western Mexico (so it wasn't in the south?) and, according to his own stammerings, had made his way by sea and land to Alamandango. That nobody, after all, was under any obligation to him. That he had gone to EARTH (that was the right word for it) in a hut on the east side of town, which he asserted was his home, had always been his home. That he could only eat things that had GROWN IN THE EARTH, potatoes, radishes, carrots, and some sorts of gourd. That Lafort had examined him thoroughly (who was Lafort?) and thought he was neither particularly human nor particularly alive. That people in the neighbourhood neither knew him nor had seen him before. That everyone should agree to turn a blind eye on the case. That it would in all likelihood never be possible to find out if he really had died a while ago in Mexico, or if he was simply trying to mystify people. That he talked (or tried to talk) of places, possessions, and women none of which had ever had anything to do with him. That he claimed to be a musicologist, but asserted also that he had made a living as a wholesale dealer, and so forth.

A few days later I drove to the east-side suburbs, left my car where the asphalt stops and the mud begins, and eventually by asking found my way to this hut. Among the drainage sluices, washing places, and shed walls daubed with political slogans in the Turkish quarter, I found a hut with a corrugated iron roof and paint-smeared windows. In it Claude sat (as usual I hesitate to give him his name) in an old garden chair. He looked more dilapidated, rotten, so to speak deader, than he had a few days earlier, so I found myself wondering how long he'd be able to go on living in this state. Did his heart work? He looked like an idol gone mouldy. Children were standing around watching as a young woman pushed watery porridge into his mouth. He recognized me at once (which gave me quite a shock), and he tried to speak.

Although I asked him to save himself the effort, he set his voice in motion with a gurgle, slow beastlike noises, the kind I already knew, and asked me for the address of a girl called Nina. I promised to find it for him and left with the children when feeding time was over. Before going back to my car, I washed my hands and face in a bar.

Two weeks later came the news that Claude had died a second time. A few Turks had done away with him (he was said to have been buried in one of the east-side cemeteries). That seemed to be the end of it. People avoided talking about him any more. But I wonder when he'll appear again, and to whom. The memory of him isn't finished and done with. He hasn't been seen again yet, but his mad craving for life (what else can it have been?) will find ways to reappear in human shape. And certainly he'll not look any less unbearable. Certainly he'll put in his reappearance at Tunifer's place.

4

— and I lived on a farm by the River Tumah. My room, whitewashed and narrow under a ceiling of heavy cross-beams, opened on a yard full of dambari trees. My job was to sweep up the leaves that had fallen during the night and to burn them behind the farm building, from which there's a view across the river toward the hill country. I swept the leaves together before daybreak and woke the birds which sat in the tree forks or lay among leaves on the ground (the constant strong wind in this region blew them at night out of the trees as they slept), and when midsummer came with hot nights and warm winds the trees in the morning were festooned with clothes, trees in the yard and trees by the river, countless trees many-hued with the clothes of loving couples who had spent the night in the hills — pants, shirts, neckties, but above all skirts, petticoats, and bodices. The wind had wrapped them around the tree trunks, they hung from the branches, dragged mixed with leaves and dust across the open clay spaces between the farm buildings, or lay crumpled in a windless corner. I kept them in my room (the local farmers paid no attention to them). On market days I would cross the river and go to the village, where I offered for sale the clothes collected during the week. Doing this I found out that mainly young people came to me, little hoods of the vicinity and shy couples, also single women, who inquired about certain clothes in an uncertain way, ready to pay any price, amused or relieved if the right articles could be found. I got rid of all the clothes, the wind fed the leaf sweeper, and as summer came to an end and the wind blew cool and clothesless from the river hills and the trees shed only leaves upon the ground, there were still a few men's jackets remaining, which I kept for myself.

One particular dress I never took to sell. I had noticed a woman who came every market day and left again without buying anything. After a few weeks I asked what dress she was looking for, and discovered that it was the dress I had kept, a white one smelling of ambergris, with a grey belt. I told her that I could get the dress but that I wouldn't sell it. She indicated that she would give me something else for the dress, and since I had every intention of being given something better than money, I arranged a rendezvous for a weekend, and she came across the river and I brought her to the farm and showed her the dress in my room, and she said it was the one she'd been looking for, and from that day I was no longer living alone in my room at the farm by the river, but here and elsewhere with a woman who owned two dresses and seemed to have no other wish than to be undressed and dressed by me.

I can't remember her face any more, and I've mislaid her body too. I can't remember ever speaking or hearing her name, also I don't know what name I was living under on the farm by the river (if there was a farm by the river, and if it was me). I remember various women in various places, but this one isn't among them (although years later I saw the dress with the grey belt lying around on various hotel beds). I don't know and never shall know how far I can trust this memory of mine, yet I've kept it — as I once kept the dress — and have given it a home in a summer when I missed the wind's blowing and perhaps love too.

5

For several years I used to read the memory columns — wants and offers — in various newspapers (limited myself to papers that appear in places where I've lived), because I still had hopes of being able to fill my gaps with time (but what

does it mean, *time*) and finally to arrange Tunifer's past, thus
my own past. Names and dates — minus persons, objects,
and without number. Colourless memories of Julka (not
Julia), but who was Julka. Julka in a black raincoat at a
restaurant table in Lisbon. Half-wild memories of Joan's
wide and dry-lipped mouth and of Julia's earrings. Memory
of an Indio standing barefoot on a street jammed with mules
and buses (I tell myself it can only have been in Guanajuato)
and selling BUTTERFLIES YOU CAN WIND UP. There must have
been something unusual about this Indio. I think I remember
him placing one of the — probably tin — butterflies in the
palm of his right hand and trying to pass it to me, while I was
looking for money in my pockets. But that's the question,
that's the point: my memory reaches as far as my own hand,
reaches the butterfly in anticipation rather than in memory,
is on the verge of taking hold of it, in order to give it to Julia
(or Julka, or Ana), and — the key, the key, something to do
with the key, that's where memory stops and directs me to
the aforementioned well with the stones in it. I've been able
to recapture a few memories, and, all things considered, it's a
relief to have them, but what a state they were in when they
were given back to me, recounted by word of mouth or in
writing. Digressions, cuts, and falsifications, which make it
hard for me to feel at home among them. Their time spent in
unconversant heads has spoiled my Julias and Julkas, ruined
my scenes. Julia, Julka, Ana, Lora, or Joan — what on earth
went on when someone else was living with them? What
sorry tricks they've been taught. What tasteless clothes
they've been stuffed into, what cheap hotels they've been
taken to for the winter nights. A potpourri of inept additions,
it's ridiculous and shaming, I must tidy things up, children
instead of mistress, backyards instead of Dutch restaurant
terraces. Ana in a small Norwegian town, dressed in orange
trousers and yellow seaboots! Ana, who never had any
seaboots and was never in Norway. It's doubtful that I shall
ever repossess these memories in such a way as to live in them
again. Already I've had to replace, that is, invent, whole
provinces — battlefields, autumn days, wedding dresses,
bedrooms, street corners, and the face of Julka, Ana, Lora.
Other faces, though, I can't rid myself of, I live with them, for
better or worse, and don't know whose they are, bug-eyed

faces, dunces' heads, all in all not very beautiful. Impossible
to push them away. It's a patchwork life, indeed it is, and the
thought that a large part of my memories (really I'd have
needed them for a life without bitterness), that the main part
of my memories has been borne away, lost, ravaged, because
the witnesses are dead, or are living in regions unattainable to
me and my newspaper advertisements! And the thought that
my past has nothing to vouch for it, an existence shrunk to a
FEW CLUES, reduced to WANTED pictures and a clutter of
anecdotes, a piffling infinity, not guaranteed, in alien heads
extinguished before the extinction of my consciousness, time
and lifetime surrendered piecemeal to spirits of confusion for
their sportspoiling games, cruelly spoiled treasures of my
memory —

6

— and woodsmoke moving sluggishly under the arched
gateways of Patzcuaro. Smell of soured wine and burnt meal.
Urine stains on walls once white, walls of colonial style
churches eroded by saltpetre. The Virgin Mary's feet piled
with flowers and stairways piled with trash. Wide plazas full
of motionless snoozing Indios. Twilit arcades full of mules,
children, musical instruments, oil bottles, and sleeping cats.
Palaces dilapidated by families of paupers, garbage, swarms
of flies, torn hammocks —
— and we heard the laughter of the card players in the
red-windowed tavern veranda where nobody but ourselves
ever seemed to eat. Heard clattering hoofs of heavily laden
mules being driven across the plazas. Listened to evening
noises from overly narrow streets and patios crammed with
people; carillons, flutes, lilting music, sleepy notes of sorrow
and happenstance; the shouts of bus drivers behind the
hotel. And we lay naked on the wide legless bed and smoked
and watched the objects sinking into the half-light, the water
canister fastened to the wall (Julia said she'd used similar
containers in Persia), the grease-spotted mirror, too small for
Julia's hair-do, the clothes thrown on the floor, the stiff
sheets, the grimy wicker chairs and the bent-wire clothes
hangers dangling on strings. We listened into the stillness of
the stuffy room and thought — I thought — probably of
nothing. And Julia got up (it can only have been Julia),

crossed the room, pushed open the shutters, leaned out of the window, and looked across the tin roof spattered with cigarette butts toward the plaza floating in the gloom of woodsmoke and twilight. She yawned and began to dress, and I got up to help her, although dressing a woman is one of the depressing things, unbearable the end of love, the disappearance of skin still hot into orderly clothes, the reverse transformation of a body into its ordinariness. Just as Julia's arms were disappearing into white materials we heard noises from the arcade beneath the window, sandals swishing over stone, running, shouts, crack-voiced angry shouts of joy, wood hitting the ground and glass shattering (probably the overturned table of the soda-water vendor at the hotel door). And we hurried to finish doing up the buttons and the bows, Julia's comb, Julia's hair, Julia's still fragrant bright hands, her high-heeled shoes, and her necklaces clicking between quick fingers like a game of marbles. And we got ready and ran down the garbage-cluttered staircase, out of the hotel and under the arcades, stumbled into a sweatily jammed throng of people, clothes, voices, beards, sombreros, knives, dogs, fruit baskets, torchlight, and dragging fumes, and Julia ran ahead of me and away from me, while I tried to hold her back, by her elbow, by her belt. She seemed to have some definite goal in view, was already far off, thrust by the crowd away into the all-consuming inextricable jumble of eyes, hands, teeth (yes, teeth). My feet slipped on a half-fried fish (it can only have been a half-fried fish). Fumes in my eyes, dogs and rotten fruit under my shoes. Julia's hair in the smoky darkness ahead of me. Julia's white blouse, still unmistakably tapered and light, replaced by a man's shirt, then by a headscarf. Julia forced out of sight, Julia lost. And I ran through the crowd calling for Julia and saw an unusually large ship's figurehead coming through the darkness at eye-level, resting on men's shoulders, hauled and shoved, head first, knocking its tailfins against columns and torches, hair stiff in the fumes, full breasts cracked and oblique (and with terror I thought again of how near the sea was, of departure, embraces, and uncertain laughter). They were heaving the wooden woman through the entrance of our hotel, painted wood scraped against plaster, splintered against the doorframe, and fell to the floor. They pushed her into the hallway, at first unlit, then flickering with torchlight, the hallway we'd just run through, dazzled, and I heard the heavy head strike the floor, heard the strokes and whizzing of axes. The crowd pushed in, blocked the entrance, people sprawling head over heels outside the latticed windows. Axe-strokes and splintering noises in the hotel interior, echoing in rooms that didn't exist, couldn't exist. And I was looking for Julia, running through crowds with my voice full of Julia, inventing Julia with my voice (it can only have been Julia). Ran through smoky and suddenly vacant arcades, among drunken Indios, knocked over a waterskin. Still calling Julia. Did not find Julia. Julia nowhere, never had been, ever. Never found Julia again. Hotel stairs filled with smoke and smashed wood. Julia, Julia. Unimaginable ships.

The Figure on the Boundary Line

February 17   Have been in Kleiber's house for several days now; it's a glorious place. More than enough of everything. Easy life. Insect screens, air conditioning, hammock, well-tended lawn. A small tennis court under trees; it's watered every day, so is the lawn. Kleiber's library. The garage. Bath with metal edging. Large property, right to the edge of the forest. Stunningly quiet. Odd, in empty rooms, the echo of my footsteps. Wonderful to think I can spend a few months here, no obligations, alone. Unquiet years falling away from me on a silent afternoon. The cries of birds early in the morning. Time makes sounds of its own; like breathing into an empty bottle. I hear them, I hear my life, I can take hold of it, it is here.

Yesterday evening immense herds of cattle being driven past the property. Bony animals, cattlemen in jeeps, with foxlike little dogs, incredibly quick. The houseboy ran out of the annexe to reassure me. The herds are being driven to the slaughterhouse in Alamandango. The dust flew up, sulphur yellow, over house and property, into the forest. Hardly gone when the houseboy began watering lawn and trees. He even washed down the walls of the house. The wet trees smelled of rotting hay. Soon all moisture had evaporated.

February 18   The houseboy seems to be fine, his name is Luis. He arranges everything, I don't have to raise a finger. Brings tea to the veranda in the morning, cleans shoes, does all the shopping, and puts back on the shelves any books I've been reading. He even managed to get some lapsang suchong tea, and herbs from France. Constant silence of the house and its surroundings. The extraordinary ease. Now and again the houseboy's footsteps in another room, or his shadow, behind a curtain vanishing. Am amazed how little his curiosity disturbs me. We laugh whenever — most often by chance — we meet. Kleiber seems to have prepared him for me, he spoils me. More than that, he reads my wishes from my looks, although I have really none, for I have everything I need, and the quiet enables me to arrange a right relation between the world and me.

February 20   Sound of birds early in the day, it usually stops during the forenoon. Heat. Luis explains everything to me, he seems to think I'm scared by unfamiliar noises. The whistling of the air conditioner, doorbell ringing, the telephone. I tried to explain to him that these sounds are nothing strange to me. Luis laughed. He seems not to believe me. I've been here ten days now, and nothing has happened. That's the incredible thing: nothing happens. I have a hold on time, and nothing happens.

February 21   Eleven days here. Noticed a man at the far end of the property, where the forest starts. He spent the whole day in the shade of the elms. Because of the distance, I couldn't identify him precisely; from far off he looks like a cattleman. I asked Luis, but he said it was just a man, and gave no further explanation.

February 22   My suitcases have arrived; for days on end I'd been spreading a net of telephone calls over railway and bus stations and hotels, and finally my luggage got caught in it, yesterday. Five porters, three suitcases. The tip was figured by porter, not suitcase. But I don't need my things here. I don't need clothes or books. Nothing I can't do without. What's necessary Luis provides, and it's not much. A sort of joy.

This figure on the property line again today. During the afternoon he came with a bottle and filled it from the tap by the veranda. I asked Luis if the man belonged to the house, but he shook his head. I wondered about that, because he's usually so forthcoming.

February 24   This man still there today. Perhaps a neighbour, or a workman, some kind of gardener? Luis says no. I took a look at him when he was walking past the library window in the morning, silently as always, to get some water.

About forty, I'd reckon. No distinguishing features. Walks calmly along, sandals, khaki trousers. All in all, inconspicuous. Unshaven, almost bearded, the face almost invisible. Calm look in the eyes, altogether relaxed, peaceful sort of person. He moves about as if he owned the place. I shouldn't bother about him, Luis seems not to. Curious that I should think about him, all the same.

I see him coming toward the house, interrupt my reading or writing, listen, when he passes the window, stand up, see him turn the corner of the house with his bottle filled, slowly he goes across the lawn and disappears among the trees. I look at him as he goes, expect him to come back, I *observe* him, as I would observe an armadillo. I see him sitting or sleeping or dozing in the shade, sometimes looking across to the house, evidently without curiosity (yes, of course, without curiosity, because almost always he sits with his back to the house). The house seems to have no meaning for him, its occupants not to interest him. If Kleiber were here, the matter would be explained easily. He seems also to spend the nights on the property line, because I saw him this morning lying there and smoking, his face half covered by a hat.

I'm observing him. What's up with me?

February 25   This morning I went into the kitchen, while Luis was making the breakfast. Sat down at the table with him, but he won't involve himself in conversation. Firmly refuses to be interested in the man. My stopping in the kitchen seemed to annoy him.

February 26   Luis says one never knows anything. There are lots of people he says. This person, like anyone else, is just passing by, he'll go away again. It doesn't matter.

Will he really go away?

Whether he will or not, it doesn't matter at all. It doesn't matter if he stays. He's a person, hasn't got a house around him, so he'll go away again.

Unless he drops dead. If he does, Luis will get rid of him, says Luis and laughs. The only person who's a nuisance is a dead person.

February 27   First thing in the morning, this person again.

I'm certain now that he has settled down on the property line. Briefly: he lives there. He seems to own nothing but his bottle. If he really does live in the bushes or beneath the trees, from now on things are clear: Luis lives in the annexe, I live in Kleiber's house, and he lives there. None of us need get in another's way. No cause for agitation. Whoever this man may be, he is discreet, I tell myself: no need to be baffled if a solitary person shows up. The natural way he moves around here may have reasons unknown to me. And those are no personal concern of mine. Of course it would be better if he came of his own accord to explain his presence and to ask Luis or me for permission, and so on. If he had a knife, a suitcase, a bicycle, even a butterfly net, some object or other, which would enable one to infer something about him, his presence would be less disconcerting. But his only possession is this bottle.

March 1   I ask myself what he lives off. Does he have food to eat? Is there somebody who looks after him, with whom he's in contact? Are there people in his background, friends, accomplices?

He's always alone but doesn't give the impression of being lonely. He has no possessions, but seems not to feel the lack of anything. He moves around in the stillness, as if he were its creature. The difficulty is that he arouses in me neither scorn nor sympathy. If I could feel sympathy for him, the thing would be simple. I would sympathize with him and so be content enough. I don't understand his independence. It bewilders me. His indifference. I don't know about it, and that draws me on. I would like to know. You can kill a person like this, but you can't force him to tell you his name.

While I was standing at the library window and observing him, Luis appeared with the tea. He laughed, when he saw me standing at the window. He seemed to want to make fun of me.

Curious situation.

March 2   He doesn't do anything, he does absolutely nothing. He sits in the shade and smokes. I've been observing him for five or six days, as he sits in the shade and smokes and sleeps.

March 3   I've realized there's nothing he needs. He has something else. But what? What is he in harmony with? Where does his peacefulness come from?

March 4   True: he does nothing. But who could tell what occupies his thoughts? His hands and legs lie in the grass, but I can't see into his head. What plans does he have? He has eyes and ears, a nose, ideas. Perhaps he took a squinny at me one morning (usually he walks very slowly past the house) and remembers me. Now he's sitting in the shade and putting his thoughts to work on me.

Exaggeration? I walked through the village so as to be thinking of something else. I bought newspapers, nuts, cigarettes, and wine. No good. I came home and before taking off my jacket stood at the library window. He was sitting beneath the tree and smoking. Where did he get the tobacco?

March 6   At noon today I asked Luis to take the man a bottle of beer, but Luis refused.

If he wants anything, let him come and get it. He, Luis, wasn't responsible for him. The person was on the outside. If he asked for a beer, one would give him a beer, or anyway consider whether or not to give him one.

Later Luis added: One could put a bottle of beer out for him. I answered that the man couldn't know, if this were done, whether the beer was being offered or just happened to be there. Someone having perhaps forgotten it. As long as he was honest, he wouldn't touch it. Luis said that if one put a plate of rice by the water tap, the man would know that the rice was meant for him. I answered that one couldn't put his food outside the house like that, the man wasn't a dog. Luis agreed. He seems to have no rooted objection to giving the man something, but he doesn't want to take it out to him, he doesn't want to go to the property line. He refuses to cross the limit of his responsibility. He'd like to see the man come and beg. Then he'd not mind giving. He wishes to be allowed to stress, Luis does, that it is his right to give. The other person should do the asking.

Quite apart from that, Luis is right, of course; the man can always come over, if he needs anything. He has legs.

March 7   I got the better of myself and paid a visit to the man on the property line. He was sitting under a tree and he looked in my direction, quite unconcerned, didn't move an inch. I sat down beside him and offered him a cigarette. He took one, nodded, drew it across beneath his nose, raised his eyebrows, obviously to indicate that he liked the smell of the tobacco. I gave him a light, and then we smoked. Neither of us said anything. I'm certainly not a shy person, but there was no conversation. Since the man said nothing, there was no reason for talk. Finally I asked him if he liked it here. He looked at me, reticently, in a friendly way, and laughed. From this I gathered that he liked the place beneath the trees. It didn't occur to me to bother him with more questions, perhaps put him in the wrong. Certainly it's better not to get too close to someone you don't know, even if it means leaving things vague. My clumsiness in this situation.

The man is so naturally present, there, beneath the trees, that I'm almost willing to get along with him. In any case he has no bad conscience, doesn't look furtive or persecuted, that sets my mind at rest. It even draws me to him. I must get used to the presence of a person who is simply there, without reason, just as I would get used to a tree. A tree! I'm beginning to see it now. Why shouldn't he live on the property line, if he behaves like a tree or a stone?

As darkness came on I stood up and said goodbye (this clumsiness again). He went on sitting, and nodded.

Luis wasn't at all friendly this evening. He noticed me on the property line and hinted that I didn't belong there. But why not?

Like a tree, like a stone.

March 8   How can I come to terms with Luis? Evidently by not bothering about the man any more. That's impossible. While he was standing by the tap this morning I called to him through the window and asked if he'd like to step inside for a moment. The man shook his head and vanished around the angle of the house. Luis was annoyed.

I don't even know what his name is.

March 10   Went to the property line today with a plate of rice and some bread. The man seemed to be glad, and while I was making up my mind whether to stand watching him or sit down beside him, he ate the plate clean, but without any hurry, at his usual quiet pace, which draws me to him so. He wiped the grease from the plate with a piece of bread and set the plate beside him on the lawn. I asked him if he had enjoyed his meal. He nodded amiably. No, he didn't only nod, he said Yes. He spoke! The way he behaved shows he was glad of the meal, but it also shows that he doesn't need rice. So whatever I do is superfluous. I'm not feeding a beggar, I shouldn't ever forget that.

Nothing disturbs his peace. There's nothing he needs. There's nothing he has resolved to do without. Impossible to make the man in any way dependent. A waste of time to try coming close to him. A living being without connections. A person who doesn't need to realize himself because he is there, and merely to exist is enough for him. Perhaps there's nothing to be done with him, his independence is perhaps meaningless, to others at least, because it seems not to be willed, but natural. But I'm drawn to the way he looks. He isn't polite. A remote friendliness.

Strange.

March 12   Relations between Luis and me are becoming more difficult, the more I get used to the man, willing, that is, to incorporate him. Luis expects me, and probably every occupant of this house (Kleiber included?), to be indifferent to any form of life exterior to certain set situations. He tolerates no transgression. In his eyes, I have no right to carry a plate of rice out to the man. If Kleiber told him to do this, he'd obey without question, but also without understanding; I suppose not, at least. I, on the other hand, as Kleiber's guest, have to occupy the house and be served by Luis, Luis will not forgive me for going outside yesterday with a plate of rice. The way he puts a glass of beer beside my plate or cleans my shoes is rebelliously careless. Soon he'll be putting overmuch salt in the rice. I told him: that little bit of rice has done the man no harm, I took it to him gladly, we've got plenty of rice. But Luis doesn't say anything. Neither houseboy nor friend.

March 13   Luis no longer has any idea what's going on in the world. I went to the property line again.

March 14   When Luis served the meal today (as always he claimed he'd already eaten), I filled a second plate and went with two plates and two bottles of beer to the property line. We ate together. Since it was hot on the lawn, in spite of dense shade, I asked the man if he'd like to come into the house with me. There's a cool room, I said, one could sit on chairs, at a table, and get more beer from the icebox. The man said No. Amiably, but firmly. No. The second word he has spoken. A gravelly voice, almost soundless. After we'd eaten, I sat there for a while. We smoked. In spite of the heat, very pleasant. My cigarettes, he has none.

When I came back into the house, there was no trace of Luis, I shouted for him. No answer. I washed the plates myself.

March 15   Everything's fine.

March 16   Luis doesn't wake me any more in the mornings. No more tea on the veranda. I make my own breakfast, which is all the same to me. I've often done so before. It's even good to have something to do. I took tea to the property line, we had breakfast in the shade, it was almost noon before I went back to the house. The man doesn't mind, isn't particularly grateful. Why should he be, he's under no obligation to ask or thank me for anything. When I asked if he'd like anything for lunch, he said it wasn't necessary (not necessary — the third time he's spoken).

What's more, I was mistaken to suppose that he occupies himself with thoughts of me or Luis, that he puts his thoughts to work on me, as I noted before. Possibly he saw me right at the start, but only saw me, no more than that. He'll have seen me at the library window and have thought: In the house up at that end of the property there's a man living, that's all right. He does what's right himself, doubtless. Does what suits him, what's necessary to him. Is that why he's so peaceful?

Like a tree, like a stone.

Like sleep with open eyes.

March 19   Have spent whole days on the property line. He has become more communicative, but not in words. Speechlessness. His eyes and hands move. He looks at me when I speak, listens, laughs, is interested, wordlessly, soundlessly, keeping an indefinite distance. Peaceful as always.

He offered me, for the first time, a cigarette. A real weed. The pockets of his coat (actually an old smock or something of the kind) are full of dried leaves. Not necessarily tobacco. Some mixture I've never encountered. He doesn't have genuine cigarettes, doesn't need them.

March 20   Found out today that Luis had been standing for hours behind the insect screen of the library window, watching me, or us. When I came back to the house toward nightfall, he fled. A reproachful look, a forlorn or rebellious gesture is all that Luis can spare for me.

March 23   Luis hasn't been shopping for days. Looked for him in the annexe. Can't find Luis.

March 25   Hard to say how the day went by on the property line. One cigarette, two. A word. Some sleep. The man is like a collection box into which time gets thrown.

Hot breath from the trees, nearness of the forest. Deep tree shade. Sounds of birds, the stillness, the smell of tobacco, the man's eyes always half-closed. Nothing happens. Like sleep. I think about this, try to, but nothing happens in my thoughts. Soundlessness. One comes to realize that time has no meaning. The constantly whirling dregs of memory are laid to rest. He seems to be dozing, but that's not the case. He's receptive to everything, he accepts everything, as long as no people and no constraints are involved. But there's no haughtiness, no hostility in this. A peacefulness that excludes the human? Like a tree, like a stone. The world comes to him. The world is there.

Luis was watering the lawn, but kept his distance and turned his back on us.

March 26   He came back today and said there was a plate of rice beside the water tap, it hadn't been touched. When I went into the house at nightfall, the plate was not there any more.

Luis sad.

March 29   Haven't seen Luis for days. Icebox empty, no more beer. Rice and all — Kleiber's supplies gradually running out.

Yesterday he asked if I was hungry. I was, and I was rash enough to say so. He went off and came back, an hour later, with bread and several oranges. I didn't ask where he got them. Bread and oranges appear, it's only natural.

April 2   He organizes things (impossible for him to go begging). Can't think of the right word just now. He provides. He went organizing on my behalf. No explanations. When I asked today where he had got the things, he laughed and said nothing. We don't eat much, one doesn't need much. Peace.

April 3   The whole day outside. Back into the house when it got dark. Luis had put the light on, so I could find my way, by the library window. Slept in my bed. Why in bed?

April 5   He's organizing again. We take turns going to the water tap.

April 6   Night spent outside.

April 12   Just came in to get some matches. Shall take Kleiber's bottles of gin too.

April 15   Am staying outside.

April 19   My first organizing trip to village. Crackers, a few oranges.

April 27   Fetched blanket, a bit cool at night.

April 29   Fetched a few blankets today.

I came home a week ago, Kleiber writes on September 15, and it took some time before I could establish the facts. If I can believe my houseboy (and I'm certain he says what he knows), an unknown man appeared one day and settled down at the end of the garden, on the property line. Henri was visibly very disconcerted by his presence. He is said to have stood for hours at the library window, observing the man. Finally he spoke to him and visited him on the property line, even took food to him. My houseboy maintains he didn't know the man. Finally Henri spent whole days in that man's company and came into the house less and less often. He took some of his clothes outside with him, also a blanket, and all the food there was, but no books, no paper, neither glasses nor saucepans nor any domestic utensils at all. He left his suitcases behind, most of his clothes and shoes, as well as his papers. I can't tell if they are all there. The houseboy swears he hasn't touched Henri's papers and possessions. He tried, he says, to keep Henri away from that man, but failed to do so. Thereafter he got ready to defend the contents of my house, if necessary with the shotgun, but Henri showed no interest in the house. Finally he never so much as entered it. Probably forgot it existed. He — the houseboy — says he saw the two men sitting and lying beneath trees day after day, evidently doing nothing. Because of the distance he couldn't hear their voices. As usual, either Henri or the other would come to the house in the morning to fetch water, but neither of them came into the house or even noticed it. The houseboy tried at first to speak with Henri, but hadn't been able to do so, because Henri hardly reacted. In a firm but not unfriendly way Henri avoided giving an explanation, or he refused any. The houseboy felt ignored. For about two months the men had lived on the property line, and to all appearances were content. Each night the houseboy had left the light on in the library, in case Henri should ever come back. One morning they had both vanished.

That's seven or eight weeks ago now. They haven't been

seen since, either singly or together. The houseboy went once to the property line but found only cigarette ends and empty beer bottles. I myself have made inquiries about Henri in every conceivable place, but haven't been able to find out anything at all. So I can only say that Henri has vanished.

How did Caravaggio die?

Do you know how Caravaggio died?

To an art historian it doesn't matter. It does matter to me. I can't sever Caravaggio's actual existence — the history of his times, his life, his death — from his pictures. He is an artist who has touched me.

Van Gogh's depressions, and the monotonous meals of Pontormo, noted in his diary each day; Max Beckmann's urbane conceit, masked, sporting a tuxedo, and George Grosz's drinking — to me these weren't insignificant. The serenity of Matisse in his old age always stuck in my mind; and de Staël's suicide, at least for me, said something about the progression of his work, his development, his method.

Then I saw Caravaggio's *David*, the hacked-off giant head in David's fist, a self-portrait of the painter when he was thirty-three, and this image hounded me into insomnia. In Rome for a few weeks I went every day to the Villa Borghese and looked at this David of Caravaggio's, this one picture. I learned it optically by heart. I've never forgotten the worn, gaping teeth, the jaw sagging and bloody, the enraged mouth of the beaten giant, gargoyle face, broken angel, barbaric innocence.

Humanity in the lavatory of Creation. Face of the Abyss. Visage of Dark Night. The *maudit*.

And I thought: This is how someone must look on the way through hell, aftermath of a life of subversion, revolt, protest; anarchy of a productive organism gone clean contrary to all the norms. The self portraits of Rembrandt, Goya, Beckmann, Van Gogh, Otto Dix — that was it. With anyone desiring less than the total view I had no patience; the lives of laureates were no concern of mine.

Caravaggio — first it was the paintings I saw in Rome, Florence, and Cleveland. Sovereign painting, compact and brilliant. Caravaggio, a great scene-designer. His technique

C. Michel   Plumplori   3/5

of illumination a fundamental discovery for painting. Insurgence of light, stormy, a thunderbolt, dangerously bleached or chill, beamed on to the palpably real, fleshly figures. No way to tell, in the religious scenes, where the saturnian light is coming from. Violent dramaturgy of the composition, but exact — David's nipple is located a little way below the geometrical centre of the picture and marks its optical centre. The Ideal Human Image no longer exists. Henceforth there are unmistakably individual faces, and bodies in action, suffering. The worm-eaten apples of his still-life, *The Fruit Basket*, were in 1600 unprecedented. The crossed legs and dirty footsoles of St Matthew shocked the ecclesiastics who commissioned the painting; they rejected this 'undignified figure'. Caravaggio disposed of the Olympian canon of figures. Into the studio he brought the street — the models for his apostles were artisans, peasants, guttersnipes, and old folk, whom he dressed up but did not beautify. Independence of a creator who disregarded the assumptions of people commissioning his work. Caravaggio was the underworld, rebellion and irony, glittering eccentricity — but he was also the biography of the first modern man in the world of painting.

Do you know how Caravaggio lived? Does that matter to the art-historian?

A furious melancholic. Scarface.

Artistic brain.

A nasty sort, an erratic character.

Criminal genius. Plutonian hoodlum. A mocker. Chaotic. A vital type. A *provocateur*.

Perhaps, in the bar-rooms, a dandy. But a dandy stylizes himself and needs time for his grooming. Caravaggio had no time for that.

Lawsuits, money — and prison sentences, insults, and actions committed in anger. Thére are court documents about fights, always fights, and serious injuries, suffered or inflicted, then a licking of wounds in a hideout provided by patrons. Murder of a certain Ranuccio Tomassoni, at a ballgame in Rome on 29 May, 1606. Wounded himself, he goes into hiding in Zaragoli, Paliano, and Palestrina.

Escapes from Rome, Naples, Malta, Syracuse, Messina,

and Palermo. He left no place in the ordinary way.

His existence — a continuous ricochet.

Skin, brain — and the commissions — all too constricting. The world, too. Caravaggio: a life in flight from prosecution. Escape from prison, changes of address, amnesty — but he can't endure peace and quiet. His known and acknowledged capabilities as a painter make him the most sought-after artist of his time. He is created a Maltese Knight (the honour is revoked after his flight) — a Cross, a gold ring, and two Muslim slaves. The scandals alternate with comparatively quiet phases of work. As a craftsman he is wholly concentrated, never makes a false move, goes straight to the point, and fast. In spite of his hounded life, there are no unfinished pictures, at most a few that are not so well painted.

After the previous self-portraits, such as the face of the Medusa with the snakes biting themselves to pieces (1600: he portrays himself with a wide-open mouth, delighted and horrific, blood by the gallon pouring from the throat), and after the *Martyrdom of St Matthew*, painted somewhat later, where he appears as a subordinate figure — the tormented physiognomy of a man whose age can't be told — Caravaggio paints his David in 1606, four years before his death. The picture is a canvas of normal size, 125 by 101 cm. The colours range from white, through grey, to brown. Total darkness of the space behind — suggestion of a curtain in it, conventional trappings of a pictorial scene, the only prop to this image, and painted with a bad conscience, it seems — and before that darkness David stands holding up the hacked-off head of Goliath, Caravaggio's self portrait, his confession. The identification of Goliath and Caravaggio turns the Old Testament story into a personal one, Caravaggio's most personal painting, most personal self-portrait. It has been said (but there can be no certainty) that David is a portrait of the young Caravaggio. If this is so, then the picture is a double portrait, a rigorous comparison between two ages in one man's life, beginning and end of a career, the barely twenty years between beauty and abnormality, gentleness and horror, compassion and rage. David holds his sword confidently, but looks sorrowful. The victor is not convinced. Remarkably quiet, taken aback: How did I arrive at this triumphal moment?

Must a victory entail slaughter?

Why victory, why defeat? Why me? Why this other person?

David seems to know his adversary. He understands his victim and is sorry for him, loves him perhaps. This is a breathtakingly deep communication, and it is the most human, intimate, creaturely picture that Caravaggio ever painted. There's no champion here, there are just two players in a tragedy. The question of guilt seems to have lost all force, but not Caravaggio's self-reproach: Who am I? Who have I come to be?

A reckoning down to the bare bones.

Tat twam asi.

Unchristian visage, saturnian, anything but that of a martyr.

The self-expression is so ruthless it transcends Caravaggio's narcissism.

It is the most unmasked self-portrait known to me.

As regards composition and texture, it is his simplest picture, and it is, as a psychogram, his most complex.

It is the death-conscious and life-reflecting finale to his existence, private and public.

Caravaggio, thirty-four years old, flees from Palermo to Naples. There he is once again involved in a fight, and is wounded. In October 1609 it is rumoured that he is dead; the rumour is false. He stays in Naples and recuperates from his wounds. On 28 July, 1610 news of his actual death reaches Rome. A report of the time runs as follows:

He was taking a few things and whatever he could still find on board a felucca bound for Rome, for he was to return there at the behest of Cardinal Gonzaga, who was treating with Pope Paul V for his pardon. On the shore (of Port Ercole) he was mistakenly seized by the Spanish crew, taken to gaol and detained there for two days. On his release, he could no longer find the felucca, so that in rage and despair he ran along the beach, beneath the might of the sun that stood in the sign of Leo, in order to see if he could still espy the ship with his things. Finally he collapsed in a place on the beach, where he lay down on a bed, having caught a bad fever, and within a few days, without help from anyone, he died a death worse even than the life he had lived.

A bad life and a bad death — that is how it would be viewed by a believer in respectable prosperity. That is how the church would think of it, and the aristocracy. What Caravaggio thought, we don't know. It is conceivable that he still thought he had lived too brightly, too innocuously. Did Villon and Rimbaud live bad lives? Did they die bad deaths? Did they consider their lives botched, badly lived, or false?

Bad, says the bourgeois, and stays inside his shelter.

Mealymouth says it, the Pharisee,the dignitary, and the bureaucrat.

The eater of dust doesn't say it. Kleist doesn't say it, nor does Clemens Brentano. Robert Walser doesn't say it. Pontormo doesn't say it and Verlaine doesn't say it. Pascin, Soutine, Gauguin, Genet, Beddoes and Lowry waste no words on it.

In rage and despair, that's the gist of it.

Not in despair at oneself, but in rage and despair at this accident that has been readying itself for a lifetime, and leads to a situation without rhyme or reason. Caravaggio made to look ridiculous, forced to assume the defensive, exposed to the sun, impotent, and finally sick to death. A condition you can do nothing about. Despair at chance. Despair that chance should lay waste his eyes and hands, despair at the anonymity of this process.

Rage against death.